THE WAY WE LIVE:

What Americans Need To Know To Govern Their Country

BY

John M. Shaw

TABLE OF CONTENTS

Acknowledgements………………………………..v

Introduction……………………………….……..vii

1. A LOOK AHEAD………………………….1

2. OUR SYSTEM AND OURSELVES………..13

3. CAPITAL…………………………………..23

4. THE CORPORATION……………………41

5. PROFIT…………………………………..53

6. MONEY……………………………………65

7. BANKS……………………………………..75

8. INFLATION…………………………….…..85

9. UNEMPLOYMENT………………………103

10. A LOOK BACK-AND A LOOK AHEAD…111

FOR FURTHER READING………………….121

Acknowledgements

I am most grateful to Professor Robert R. Ebert of Baldwin Wallace College, the first person to take the idea of this book seriously. He offered many suggestions that were a great help to me.

I also am indebted to the late Professor Milton Friedman, Senior Research Fellow at the Hoover Institution, for his generous help to me in obtaining necessary data for Chapter 8. It would have been impossible for me to make the point that inflation is a monetary phenomenon more clearly than he already had done.

"People who mean to be their own
governors must arm themselves
with the power which knowledge gives."

James Madison
1751 – 1836
Fourth President of
The United States

"We owe it to our ancestors to preserve entire those rights,
which they have delivered to our care: we owe it to our
posterity, not to suffer their dearest inheritance to be destroyed."

The Letters of Junius
No. 20
August 8, 1769

Introduction

To the Reader: Why Bother?

About 30,000 years ago, a man was standing in a meadow near a forest in what is now central Europe. He was naked. He wasn't doing anything, because there wasn't anything to do. He was just standing there. After a while, the man felt hungry, so he walked over to a bush and picked and ate some berries. Then he stood some more.

As he was standing there, the sun disappeared behind the trees. The air grew chilly, so the man picked up an animal skin he had dropped on the ground earlier in the day when it was warm. At some time in the past, he had killed an animal for its meat and then removed its hide. He wrapped the skin around himself and stood some more.

Gradually, darkness closed in, and the sky became overcast. It started to rain, so the man walked to a cave not far from where he had been standing. He entered it and squatted before a small fire with several others who already were there, some older, some younger, some female. No one spoke.

It was the end of another day, the same as the day that had preceded it, the same as the day that would follow it. Life was not elegant, and at times it was not easy. But it was understandable. What you saw was what there was, and you could see and understand everything.

The passage of some 300 centuries, from that distant day in prehistoric central Europe to twenty-first-century America, has, of course, left our basic needs unchanged. Like the man in the meadow, we still need food, clothing, and shelter. But unlike the man who got what he needed directly by walking only a few feet from spot to spot, we today live and work in a very large and highly developed economic system to satisfy our basic needs. Also, when the man in the meadow got his food, clothing, and shelter, he had obtained everything there was to be had. His life was one of simple survival and no more. Americans today, on the other hand, live in an advanced country and have available to them all of those goods and services that characterize a modern society.

This book explains the operation of the American economic system, and in a sense, it's a little like an owner's manual for a power lawn mower or a home appliance. It's not going to tell you about every little gear and bolt in the American economic "machine," but it will tell you enough about how it works so you can

1. Understand what our economic system is.

2. Understand what it is supposed to do for you.

3. Make sure that it stays in good working order.

Why bother learning anything at all about the way we live? For two reasons. First, because in America, "We the people of the United States...," (to quote the Preamble of our Constitution) are the ones who set the rules for how our economic system should operate. We live in a democracy, so we do that through our political system when we vote and when we communicate with our elected representatives. That actually is how we determine our standard of living and our quality of life. We need to understand how our system works because we're not merely a part of it, we're in charge of it, and we can't alter that fact any more than we can alter the law of gravity.

We, therefore, have a choice to make: Either we understand our system and control it ourselves, or we don't. It's a simple choice, it's our choice as Americans, and it's a choice we must make.

Capitalism is an economic system based on freedom, our natural human state.

But as true as all of that is, there is another very compelling reason to become familiar with the basic workings of our American economy. It's not just that we have had this honorable obligation thrust upon us. It also is to our definite and distinct *personal* advantage to take an interest in, learn about, participate in, and maintain our control over our economic system. Why? Because it already has done so much real, measurable, visible good for us, and for the rest of the world, that we would be very foolish indeed—almost to the point of being self-destructive—to let the control that really is ours slip away from us.

Our economic system is called capitalism, and it is based on freedom, our natural human state. Capitalism came into being not because it was specifically and consciously established by our country's Founders. Capitalism came about because it was the only economic system that could possibly develop from the cherished and hard won political freedoms that *were* specifically and consciously established by our country's Founders.

America's Founders were truly amazing people. They possessed qualities that are found only rarely in any people, in any place, at any time, in the long history of the world. And that worked out very well, because what they had before them was a situation and set of circumstances that had never before been encountered by any other people, in any other place, at any other time, in the long history of the world.

But even more importantly, they saw what was before them as not just another problem that they had to solve or some sort of a pain in the neck that they had to deal with as quickly as possible so they could get back to their own personal lives. They saw it as an opportunity, a great and grand opportunity, to do something that had never before been done. And they seized it, with glorious enthusiasm.   With total commitment. Nothing half-hearted about it:

> "And for the support of this Declaration [of Independence], with a firm reliance on the protection of Divine Providence, we mutually pledge to each other our Lives, our Fortunes and our sacred Honor."

They laid it *all* on the line.

America's Founders understood that they had a chance to establish, from scratch, a brand new country that would be based on principles that would allow people to be truly free. Those principles would come from ideas that had been talked and written about for a long time but that had never before been acted upon and put into practice in any significant way. They furthermore had a chance to apply these ideas not just to a small group or community of people, and not just in a gradual fashion, but to an entire country, and all at once. Clean slate. Out with the old, and in with something that was totally and completely new. And this is where their rare qualities came in and really showed themselves:

> They had the courage and the inspiration to write the Declaration of Independence.

> They had the strength and the fortitude to fight the American Revolution till they had won on to victory.

> They had the ability to recognize and provide for each individual's separate worth and place in the world, with a true understanding of the working of the human spirit, which led to the creation of our Constitution.

From all of that—inevitably and unstoppably—came the freedom and the benefits of capitalism, as "We the people of the United States..." became sovereign masters of our own country, because we would be, first and foremost, sovereign masters of our own lives. Our government would be one "...deriving [its] just powers from the consent of the governed...." (The Declaration of Independence again.) We would be free to build our country into the best thing that it could be, because we would be free to go about our own daily lives, doing our personal best to provide ourselves and our families with what we needed to live.

And that is where capitalism came from.

Nowhere else in the world and at no other time in history has there been a political system like ours and a set of economic arrangements that flows so naturally from it and works so well with the basic drives that are an integral part of our human nature, that allows everyone in it to be free to maximize his talents and capabilities, and then rewards him for doing it. And that's a very good way to do things. All we have to do is to look around us and see how ordinary people live here, where capitalism lives and moves and has its being, and then look elsewhere around the world to see how ordinary people live where it does not.

But hardly anyone in America thinks of that kind of thing these days, and it's not because we're stupid or shortsighted or selfish. Why then? The reason is that hardly anyone alive in this country today ever has known anything other than a prosperous America. This truly is a land of plenty, even in the most difficult times: Katrina in New Orleans, 9/11 in New York, massive earthquakes in Los Angeles, Sandy on the East coast. Whatever. The truth is that we have not merely enough to enjoy the good times, but plenty and to spare to get through the bad.

Unfortunately, however, because our country has been doing so well for so long, we have come to regard our prosperity the same way that we regard gravity: It's just there, it's never going to go away, and that's all there is to it. But that is, most emphatically, *not* the case. We must guard our economic freedom with the same vigilance with which we guard our personal and our political freedom. It is, after all, our economic freedom that makes it possible for us to produce the abundance that is ours and the prosperity that makes us the envy of the world. But to guard it properly and effectively and preserve it in good working order, we must understand it. There's no other way. But Americans—as a people, as a country—are largely unfamiliar with the system that we use to produce everything we have, because economics, as it affects the everyday affairs of working Americans, has become a largely untaught subject in our schools.

> *Compassionate aid is one of our country's*
> *leading exports. America helps people.*

People understand political freedom pretty much instinctively, but because we don't fully understand the role that economic freedom plays in our lives, we don't see how it can slip away from us and how and why that is impacting our political freedom and the quality of our lives on a day-to-day basis. Milton Friedman, Nobel prize winner and one of the most influential and productive economists of the twentieth century, explained it this way: "Economic arrangements play a dual role in the promotion of a free society. In the first place, freedom in economic arrangements is itself a component of freedom broadly understood, so economic freedom is an end in itself. In the second, economic freedom is also an indispensable means toward the achievement of political freedom."

We furthermore not only do well for ourselves, we backstop the rest of the world. No matter where tragedy or misfortune strikes in this world, aid from America is there, and not just in token or symbolic quantities. We also have a long-standing and solidly established record of helping friend and foe alike: The Soviets and their short grain harvests, victims of floods, tsunamis, hurricanes, and any other kind of natural disaster the world over. We've even offered aid to North Korea.

In fact, it can be fairly said that compassionate economic aid is, and has been for something like three quarters of a century now, one of our country's leading exports. America helps people. All you have to do is go back to the middle of the twentieth century.

In 1945, at the end of World War II, Europe lay in ruins. The Allies had emerged victorious, but even more importantly for the future of Europe, and for the future of the world, the United States was intact. Uncle Sam may have been mopping his brow a bit, but he was on his feet and standing tall at that. America bestrode the world.

What had made that victory possible primarily was the industrial strength of our capitalist economic system. (Just as it was the North's industrial and economic strength that preserved the Union and ended slavery a century earlier.) No other country could have done it. Once America shifted gears from the manufacture of consumer goods to the production of war materiel, we were able to arm ourselves and our allies in a couple of years and then go on to win the war in three years more, even though the Nazis had been gearing up for war for several years before that. (During that time, incidentally, we produced not only the guns that were needed but nearly all of the butter we were accustomed to during peacetime. There were some temporary shortages, but no privation.)

None of this, of course, is to ignore the tremendous cost in human life that was borne by both America and its partners. It simply recognizes that all of the bravery and human suffering would have been in vain had it not been for America's ability to arm the Allies. But as good as all of that was, there would be more, much more.

When the strife was o'er and the battle done and America had saved the world from Hitler (and Tojo), we didn't just dust off our hands, say "You're welcome," and go home. Americans still had not only the material wealth but the human compassion as well to implement the Marshall Plan to rebuild as much of Europe as we were able to help. (The Soviets "helped" Eastern Europe in a different way.) We put $12 billion into that effort, a huge sum at that time, and not exactly pocket change today.

Through the Marshall Plan, the world saw the human spirit at its best, at its most politically free, at its most economically strong, at its most humanly compassionate. The world saw capitalist America.

The Marshall Plan (officially, the European Recovery Plan) was proposed by and named for General George C. Marshall, Chief of Staff of the Army during World War II and later Secretary of State. "Its purpose," he explained, "should be the revival of a working economy in the world so as to permit the emergence of political and social conditions in which free institutions can exist."

Recall what Milton Friedman said a few paragraphs ago about political and economic freedoms being so closely tied together. Almost a matter of two sides of the same coin.

But it's more than the money that is both note- and praiseworthy. It's the fact that we still not only were able but willing as well to do it after five-years on a war footing. It was an excellent showing both for the economic system itself and for the people using it. Through the Marshall Plan, the world saw the human spirit at its best, at its most politically free, at its most economically strong, and at its most humanly compassionate. The world saw capitalist America.

It was our economic system, free, robust, and productive, that allowed America to have the wherewithal that was indispensable to be a true and an effective world leader.

What happened during and immediately after World War II is only one example. There are many more, but that one set the tone of world history for the next half century. No other country, nothing less than capitalism, as applied and practiced in America, could have equipped the Allies to rescue the world and preserve the freedom we enjoy today. No other country could have been the Arsenal of Democracy.

Here is another example of the beneficial working of capitalist freedom in a free democratic society. It definitely is neither understood nor appreciated for what it is, but in its own way, it is just as powerful and contributory to our well-being on an ongoing and day-to-day basis.

A man died in 2012, and America, and much of the rest of the world, wept. Steve Jobs was not merely respected and admired. He was truly beloved, because he had done so much good for so many people. Plain old ordinary people. He had made their lives better, more productive, more satisfying. More fun.

Sure, the better mousetrap will make the inventor successful, but the real payoff for any society is that better mousetraps catch everyone's mice, and that way everyone is better off.

How did he do it? Steve Jobs was able to do what he did because he was able to pursue his own self-interest in a free-market capitalist economic system. That, by and large, is pretty generally understood. But what is not well or widely understood is the fact that that is only the first, and the less important, part of it. Way more important for society as a whole is that millions of people were able to use and benefit from what Steve Jobs had done because they, too, were living in the same economic system, the same country in which he lived and worked and accomplished and flourished. And that is a much bigger deal when you consider things on the basis of benefit per capita. Very possibly, in fact very likely, many of the most dedicated and committed anti-capitalist Occupiers, on Wall Street and elsewhere, not only were among the mourners but were beneficiaries as well of what he had done. (A sort of mass cognitive dissonance?)

What they're missing is that sure, the better mousetrap will make the inventor successful and prosperous, but the real payoff for any society is that better mousetraps catch everyone's mice, and that way everyone is better off. But the Occupiers just didn't seem to understand that, to be fully aware of why that was and how it happened.

Of course it's not always obvious, and we can't always see each and every clever little thought that comes along. We can't watch what happens from the time something pops into someone's head until it works its way through the system and finally is put to use in a better home appliance or audio system or piece of manufacturing equipment. But what we can see—because it's all around us—is what happens in a country in which good ideas are encouraged, used, and rewarded. It's what happens when the human spirit and human intelligence and smartness simply are let alone and allowed to function freely. It's what happens in America.

Then there's the government's opinion:

Toward the end of 2014, the media devoted a good bit of attention, and rightly so, to something that was said by one of the architects of the Affordable Care Act (Obamacare). These are the words of Jonathon Gruber, a professor at the Massachusetts Institute of Technology who was paid $400,000 for his part in the development of the ACA:

"Lack of transparency is a huge political advantage. And basically, call it the stupidity of the American voter or whatever, basically that was really, really critical for the thing to pass."

Take those words personally, because whether you actually are a voter or not, they are about you. They are about *all* Americans. And that wasn't just a careless, isolated, slip-of-the-tongue misstatement. It was a rare and candid revelation of how so many of the people in and around government, who are supposed to be working *for* us and have derived their just powers *from* us, actually think *of* us. They actually believe that we are mentally incapable.

But even that stunning admission didn't get it right. We're not stupid. Stupid people never could have accomplished all that we have accomplished here in America. If, on the other hand, Gruber had said that

Americans are habitually inattentive and complacent, he would have been correct. This was said earlier, but again, it bears repeating: America has been doing so well for so long that we just take our prosperity and our high standard of living for granted. We regard our ability to produce easily and efficiently the things that keep us safe and comfortable the same way we regard gravity: The stuff is just there, it's never going to go away, and that's all there is to it. But that is not so. Not so at all. We Americans have done tremendous things. The reason is that we are free to put our basic human smartness to work in our own self-interest and to strive to do our best for ourselves and our families.

We'd be very foolish indeed to let it all go to pot simply because we don't understand how this marvelous system of ours not only works, but works for us.

So that, very briefly, is why it's worth a modest amount of time and effort to become familiar with the way we live. It's not all theoretical. There is some real incentive to which each and every one of us can relate personally in our own lives. There is real motivation. There is something real and good for each one of us: There is our own personal day-to-day freedom and well-being to think of and consider seriously.

The only way our country, as a nation, can remain free is for each of us, individually, to remain free, both politically and economically.

And that is what this book is about: Our personal freedom as Americans.

The true test of any economic system is how well those living and working in it are able to provide for themselves and their families.

1 A Look Ahead

Americans live better than anyone else in the world. That's not an arrogant boast, and it's not a confession of shame or guilt. It's just a simple statement of fact. We are the most prosperous country on earth and we have the highest standard of living in the world, which means that in the ordinary day-to-day business of providing ourselves and our families with what we need to live, we are more successful than anyone else. As the song says, nobody does it better.

But why? What's so different about Americans that makes us so much better at producing things for ourselves? The answer, in a word, is nothing. Americans are, after all, just people from all over the rest of the world (or their descendants) who happen to be living on the lower half of the North American continent. The thing that makes the difference is not who we are but how we do things. It's our system. It's simply the best there is. Again, not a boast. Just another statement of fact.

The reason that ours is the best system for the production of goods and services is that it works so well with one of the strongest and most basic reflexes in human nature: The reflex that makes us automatically, almost unconsciously, try to figure out a simpler, easier, and generally better way of doing things. Because once someone has come up with a better way, our economic system not only permits but encourages that individual to apply it—and then offers a reward for putting it to use. *That's* how a country's standard of living rises, and it's the basic idea, provided for in the U.S. Constitution, behind patents and copyrights: Reward for the individual who not only has come up with a good idea but who has pursued that idea, worked hard, and produced something new, something better that didn't exist before.

> *The thing that makes the difference is not*
> *who we are but how we do things. It's our system.*
> *It's simply the best there is.*

And that plays into another of the strongest and most basic reflexes in human nature-- The motivation to act that comes from the incentive of personal gain: Maybe I can have something better for myself and my

1

family if I work at this idea of mine. And if the achievements of this country in a mere two and a half centuries of political and economic freedom don't demonstrate the power of personal incentive to accomplish good things in this world, nothing can.

That's why Marxism, in the Soviet Union or anywhere else, never succeeded and certainly never gave those living under it anything close to the kind of life we have here in America. Not only did it not work with human nature, it actively worked against it. We here in America believe in, and have codified into our laws, what we believe are our "unalienable Rights." (See the Declaration of Independence.) Among them is the right to private property and the right to feel secure about the property we own. (The fourth amendment to the Constitution.) That really is a very big deal, and although every American would agree that it is, most of the time we just take it for granted. But when Karl Marx was asked what Communism's ultimate goal was, he said simply, "Abolition of private property." Combine that with atheism, which was official government policy, and what are you offering a person? Nothing in this life and no next life at all. The true wonder of the Soviet Union is that it lasted as long as it did.

The complete picture of a country's standard of living, however, is found not only in such cold statistics as, say, the number of flat-panel HDTVs per household. It is, in fact, found mainly in the security and the peace of mind that come to a people when they are well past a hand-to-mouth existence, when they can do better for themselves as a nation than merely survive.

The attainable level of human contentment in America is quite high. Our quality of life is good. The reason? We are free, both politically and economically. We live in a good country.

Our American economic system, capitalism, under which we live and work and have done so well for ourselves, is possible because of our political system, which, in the end, is based on the idea of maximum responsible freedom for the individual.

2

Bernie and the Illegals

(No, it's not a rock group.)

You can learn a lot watching other people, even when their behavior is pretty bad, provided that you know what you're looking at and understand what you're seeing.

Bernie Madoff was a crook and a predator and a liar and just an all round bad guy. If you want any more than that, and there's plenty, you can Google him. He swindled thousands of people out of billions of dollars. One thing he wasn't, however, was dumb. But to understand why he is significant here, it is helpful to go back to the first half of the twentieth century, say the 1930s and 1940s, to another crook named Willie Sutton.

Willie was a bank robber, and he was a very colorful guy. He was known as Willie "The Actor" Sutton, because he so frequently used disguises in his work. Someone once asked him why he robbed banks. His answer? "Because that's where the money is."

And that is what Bernie Madoff understood so well and appreciated so happily about America. This is where the money is. That's why he decided to set up shop right here in his own back yard. He could have gone anywhere in the world to work his schemes. So what if he couldn't speak Spanish or Greek or French? There are bilingual crooks the world over, and he could have partnered with any of them. But he didn't. He worked at home, because America is where the money is.

Sure, there's wealth in other countries, but there's not enough of it, and what there is, is not in the hands of enough separate people. America is unique in the world. Not only is there money here but it's money that's spread out. It's widely distributed, not just in the hands of a few families at the top of our society. The Occupiers were wrong. America's prosperity is broadly based. Sure there are a few people at the top with a lot. There always are in any country. But what is different about America is that there is this huge, prosperous middle class. That's where you find savings accounts and mutual funds and IRAs and 401Ks. These things are all over the place, not just in the hands of a few. Bernie saw America as the fertile ground that it is, and he plowed it like an eager farmer in springtime.

And the illegals? Three quarters of the world's emigration doesn't come to America's shores and cross its borders, legally or otherwise, because they're looking for a harder and more disciplined life. Those doting Central American parents didn't send their children south to Brazil. It's America that draws them all, because we're the best there is, and the rest of the world knows it. What is not understood, including by a lot of us, is how we got to be the best and what made it all possible. And that's what this book is about.

Capitalism emphasizes three principles:

1. Private ownership of property, including the means of production.

2. Dominance of the consumer, who is free to buy or not buy, as he or she pleases.

3. Individual reward for the producers of those products that please the consumer.

This book is going to examine our capitalist economic system, especially as it relates to working Americans, no matter what kind of work they do, and that covers a lot of ground. Working Americans are professionals, customer service reps, skilled trades workers, technicians, managers, corporate CEOs, clerks, production workers, entrepreneurs operating independent businesses, and homemakers managing their households. Understanding how our economic system relates to working Americans is vitally important because working Americans also are voting Americans, and it is through our political system that we control everything, including the rules for the operation of our economic system. This was mentioned in the introduction, but it's worth a brief mention here as well. It's important.

Here are a few short summaries of what's ahead.

Chapter 2. Our System and Ourselves

There is an awful lot to the United States of America. Our economy generates in the neighborhood of $15 trillion dollars per year of goods and services. Where does it all come from? One way or another we produce it. Either we make it ourselves, or we trade with other countries to obtain it. Where does it all go? One way or another, we consume it. Either we use it ourselves, or we trade it to other countries for things they make.

How is it possible for us to have so much? Adequate natural resources, of course, help. But the main reason is that the economic arrangements that we have been free to make, voluntarily among ourselves, more than any other set of arrangements anywhere else in the world, give Americans both the freedom and the incentive to maximize their physical and mental output. We do that through the use of tools, by cooperating and specializing, and finally by voluntarily trading what we produce for what we need. The result of our economic freedom, which is ours thanks to our unique Constitutional political freedoms, is the abundance—both material and nonmaterial—that comes from the free working of the American economy.

That is the true strength of our country and the source of America's greatness: The politically free human spirit at liberty in our capitalist economic system.

As a nation, we are able to provide ourselves with not just a sufficient today but with a better tomorrow—in other words, a rising standard of living and an improving quality of life.

Chapter 3. Capital

Give a person a job to do—any job—and the first thing he'll think of is, What tools do I need? It's almost a reflex. If there are no tools already available, he'll try immediately to figure out a way to make whatever tool is needed. In fact, one of the things that humans do more often and better than anything else is to design and make tools.

"Capital" simply is a word that is used when we talk about the tools—or about the money it takes to buy them—that we use on our jobs to earn a living. Those tools make it possible for us to raise our standard of living by enabling us to raise our productivity, the amount of goods we can produce with a given amount of human effort.

Increased productivity, however, whether at the individual or at the national level, does not mean "back to the sweatshops." What it means is picking up where human sweat and effort leave off and making greater use of tools—capital—to help us produce more and then live better as a result of our more productive efforts.

In the past, when most of us lived on our own farms, the saving for, acquiring, and using of tools to provide for ourselves and our families were personal activities that were carried out by the individual or the individual family. It was all right there in front of us. Today, the connection between our standard of living and our ability to acquire the tools that we all use on our jobs is not as obvious as it once was, but it is no less real. The tools that contribute to our rising standard of living and improve our quality of life today are in the factories and offices in which we work, instead of in our own fields and barns, but the way in which tools affect our lives is greater today than at any other time in human history.

In fact, it is one of the great ironies of our time that even though we depend more today on tools, capital, than ever before, we can't really see, as individuals, how we as a nation accumulate that capital. We can't see firsthand how we acquire and organize the tools that we use every day on our jobs and what the use of those tools really means to us. Our system, capitalism, works so well with the very nature of the human spirit that it is nearly invisible.

Chapter 4. The Corporation

The use of tools on an individual or a family basis makes possible a tremendous increase in productivity and a corresponding rise in living standards. Achieving the maximum benefit from tools, however, requires that we pool our resources on a large scale; specialize; work together to produce what we need; and then divide the output. The individual's share from such an arrangement always is greater than his total individual output would be, because the large pie that we all produce together is far greater than the sum of all of the small individual pies that we would produce working alone.

Capitalism is the most effective way of putting new and better ideas at the disposal of a whole nation of working men and women.

The voluntary arrangement that we use to produce most of our goods and services is the corporation. The reason that a corporate arrangement is able to produce so much more is that individual employees can be supplied with a greater quantity of capital—tools—to work with and produce with than they ever could accumulate on their own.

That is capitalism's greatest contribution to our society: It is the most effective way of putting new technology, new and better ideas, at the disposal of a whole nation of working men and women, to make their

6

lives, on the job and at home, as well as the lives of their families, less physically draining and hence better, happier, more rewarding and satisfying, more dignified and fulfilling. That is how capitalism works for the working American.

Thomas Jefferson once said that the happiness of the domestic fireside is the first blessing of Heaven, but if you are so totally exhausted when you get home from work that you can't see straight, you and your family aren't going to be spending much quality time together.

The purpose of the stock market is to help us gather the huge quantity of tools needed by a work force of over 155 million people. By means of the stock market, savers allow companies to use their money to acquire tools. The attraction to the savers is the expectation (but not the guarantee) of a payment from the corporation for the use of their savings. Those payments are called dividends.

Chapter 5.   Profit

Profit simply is the money that is left over after all current expenses of an organization have been subtracted from all of its income. That is true, whether you are talking about a giant corporation or the neighborhood dry cleaner or anyone else.

Profits serve three purposes:

1. They are a source of saveable money to acquire tools.

2. They are a means of communication between buyer and seller. If they exist, they are a sign of consumer approval of a product. If there are no profits or insufficient profits, the company is forced to take the hint from the consumer and change its product.

3. Because they are a means of communication that cannot be ignored, profits also allow the consumer to exert direct, rapid and sometimes fatal control over the producers of goods and services. The story of the Edsel and the Mustang, related in Chapter 5, provides convincing proof of this.

Profits are the ultimate, the final consumer hotline.

Besides being a source of direct savings for a company, profits also are used to attract the savings of individuals. Again, that is the purpose of dividends.

In anticipation of earning a profit, companies put forth a tremendous amount of effort to bring to the market products and services that they hope consumers, who are free to spend or not spend, will buy. The result of that effort is the huge quantity and almost limitless variety of goods and services that we see around us, that are available to us.

(A huge number of choices is available to Americans as consumers, that is. When we function as voters, however, in political matters, things are very different. Our choices, by the very nature of the political process, are much more limited. That's not bad, and it's not good. It simply is the natural difference between a political approach and an economic approach to allowing free people to make choices.

For example, there are for sale in this country automobiles from over two dozen manufacturers, who offer consumers over three dozen automobile makes. That's a lot of choice. When we enter a polling place, however, our choices are much more limited. Very often, there are only two candidates for an office. One wins, the other loses. And sometimes, elections are close. And if you're talking about a close presidential election, that means that about half of the Americans who voted in the world's leading democracy didn't get what they asked for.

Or if you're talking about an issue, our votes decide whether it passes or fails. That's it. We get two choices and no more.

Consider the referendum in Scotland in September 2014. The question was whether Scotland should remain part of the United Kingdom or become a separate country. The vote was 55% to stay with the U.K., and 45% to break off. That was no squeaker. Ten percentage points is a decisive margin. But what it also meant is that, again, nearly half the voters in a democracy wound up having to settle for something that they didn't want. Nearly half. That's a lot.

8

But it's the kind of thing people *don't* get when they can vote with their dollars. Only two automobile makes available? Ridiculous. Or two kinds of breakfast cereal? Absurd. That's the advantage to free-market solutions to what people want, and the downside to political solutions: Many choices vs sometimes only two, both of which may be unappealing.

So what's the point? Make as many decisions as possible by the free-market process. Use the political process only when necessary, just to set the rules of the game and then to see that those rules are followed by everyone. Then leave things up to the individual to make choices, to live in freedom.

But enough of this for now. More in Chapter 5.)

Chapter 6. Money

Money is a tool that we use to convert our effort on our jobs into a form that we can use to acquire what we need to live. It is a tool that we use to measure the value of the effort we put forth and the value of the things we buy. But most importantly, money is a tool that allows us to store up and save and accumulate the stuff that we have produced today but don't need to use today. It is this last job that money does for us that makes possible the great human progress that we are able to achieve.

Money is the most useful tool we ever have devised.

For all of those reasons, maintaining the steady value of our money is essential to our individual well-being on a day-to-day basis. The reason is that the real value of money to us is in what we can get for it. If your income doesn't change and if you can get two pairs of shoes for forty dollars one day and only one pair the next, you obviously are less well off because a change in the value of your money won't allow you to buy as much.

What would cause the value of your money to change? The answer to that question lies in the fact that there is a direct connection between the amount or quantity of money in circulation, compared to what there is to buy, and the value or worth of each individual piece of money.

Chapter 7. Banks

Money is a tool that enables us to sell what we produce and to buy what we need. As we all work from day to day, however, and produce more products, we need correspondingly more money to do our buying and selling. That is where banks come in. While we're all out on our jobs producing goods and services, our commercial banking system is producing something—in fact, the one thing—that we need but can't produce ourselves: Money.

How is that new money put into circulation in the economy? Through the loans that are made to both consumers and businesses, to you and to your employer.

Chapter 8. Inflation

When we talk about inflation, we are talking about a steady and relatively rapid increase in prices—the number of our dollars that are required to buy a certain quantity of goods and services.

As you know from your own experience, when prices rise, you are forced to change the way you live. That's the bad news. The good news is that inflation and the federal government are connected, and in this country of democratic government and free elections, you control—indeed you are—the federal government. Our government—that is, the bureaucracy—is one that "…[derives its] just powers from the consent of the governed." (Again, the Declaration of Independence.)

Chapter 9. Unemployment

As destructive and harmful as inflation is to wage earners, there is something else that is even worse: No wage at all. If it ever has happened to you, you know what it is to be working one day and not working the next. You were unemployed, and that was it.

But a strange thing happens when you begin to move from an out-of-work individual to the national unemployment figures that are published each month by the federal government. All of a sudden you start to see in those figures a lot of people who were *not* thrown out of work through no fault of their own. In fact, some people are hardly inconvenienced at all by being out of work. Yet, there they are, lumped right in with the rest and counted as "unemployed." Who are these people? We'll look at the statistics and see.

Chapter 10. A Look Back—And a Look Ahead

In the last chapter of this book, after we've looked at what we're doing and how we do it and what we've accomplished so far, we'll step back and see what the future might hold for us.

That's a quick overview of what's coming up next, in Chapter 2, we'll look at Our System and Ourselves.

The American economy is nothing more—and nothing less—than the sum of all of the activity of all working Americans as they go about the business of providing themselves and their families with what they need to live—food, clothing, and shelter—plus all of the other things they purchase in addition to what is needed for bare survival: television sets, automobiles, washers and dryers, lawn mowers, computers, vacations, jogging shoes, and on and on.

2 Our System and Ourselves

As working Americans look around them today, they see a huge quantity, a tremendous variety of goods and services available to them. This is an abundant land. It's a land of plenty. Even in difficult times, the truth is that there is enough. In fact, it is impossible for us to seriously imagine entering a supermarket and finding only bare shelves, or walking into a department store and finding no goods for sale. It didn't just "happen," though. We didn't just step outside one day and find it all there. Everything that we have is there because "We the people…," have worked to produce it all, using our hands and our heads and especially the tools we have saved for and devised.

But even more important to the way we live from day-to-day than the material things that we can see and touch—in fact, what makes it possible for us to produce our material abundance —is the economic system that we have inherited and now must preserve and maintain. It is through that system that we produce all that we have. It's a huge and highly developed system with a workforce of over 155 million people supplying a population of over 300 million people. And that's only the domestic market. Considering, therefore, the quantity and variety, the relative complexity, and just the sheer size of all that there is around us, it is neither wasteful nor foolish to take a good close look at the way we live.

Our lives are based on six fundamental principles:

1. Human life requires human effort. In other words, we all have to work for a living.

2. The human effort that we put forth—the work that we do—amounts to taking what we find in nature and changing it in some way to provide ourselves with the food, clothing, and shelter that we need. The reason such changing is necessary is that hardly anything we require can be found in nature in usable form.

3. When we divide up the job of providing for ourselves into smaller parts, specialize, and then assemble all of the individual contributions by trading and exchanging with each other, we can live better. The total

13

cooperative group output becomes much more than what the simple sum of all of the separate individual outputs would be.

4. When we use tools to help us work, we can accomplish more and live better, because tools allow us to multiply our human effort.

5. The basic job that any tool does for us is to change some form of energy into useful work. By doing that, a tool increases what we can produce with our effort in a given time. It makes us more productive.

6. There is such a thing as private property.

Those six principles have applied throughout history, and they apply today. No matter where the human race has been as it has developed and progressed, individuals have had to put forth some sort of effort in order to live; they have had to change what they found in nature; people have produced more by pooling their efforts and cooperating than by working alone; they have accomplished more, and have lived better as a result, when they have used tools; they always have used tools to convert some sort of energy—including their bodily energy—into useful work.

And the object of it always has been to acquire for personal use what is necessary to sustain life.

Go as far back as you like. The cave dweller in the Stone Age, for example, had to put forth effort to feed himself. Animals had to be tracked and killed for meat. Wild fruits at least had to be picked. As those things were found in nature, either on the hoof or on the tree, they were not in a form that was useful to people.

Occasionally, when people hunted together, they found they could tackle a larger animal. When even such a simple tool as a club or a spear was used to hunt, or perhaps a stick or a pole was used knock down fruit from high tree branches, people gathered food a little more easily, and they ate a little better. They were using tools to help them with their work, which at that time was just getting enough to eat.

14

The job that the club or the spear did was to change the energy in the hunter's arm into a form that would help him catch the main course for his dinner. The stick transferred energy from a human arm that was close to the ground to a branch that was several feet up so a piece of fruit could be knocked down. And of course, the individual either kept or shared in whatever was caught or picked.

Eventually, about 5,000 B.C., people began to help nature along. They started to raise animals for food and to tend and cultivate crops. But even with that great change, a lot of the work still was carried out very much on an individual or a family basis. You provided primarily for yourself and your family, occasionally working with someone else. You used tools to convert energy, but it was no more than your own personal human energy working a primitive digging stick. But even so, you were able to live a little better.

A giant step

Then things changed dramatically. What happened was that about 4,000 B.C., farming got really good. The development of a simple plow that was pulled by oxen was the main reason, and people were able to grow much more than they needed—more than they needed to live from day-to-day and more than they needed just for themselves. That meant that some people who wanted to try their hands at other things could do so, and they traded what they produced to the farmers for food. Four things happened as a result:

1. Not all individuals or individual families supported themselves completely and directly from beginning to end.

2. People began to specialize.

3. Trade—or commerce or business or whatever you want to call it—entered the scene.

4. There was, very shortly, the need for, and the development of, something called "money."

And so things remained for nearly six thousand years until two things happened, two of the most important events in the history of the world. The first was that in 1775, James Watt put the finishing touches on the steam engine. That meant that tools could be developed that would run on steam power and could convert—and in a big way at that—something other than muscular energy, either animal or human, into useful work. That, in turn, meant large machines, conversion of natural resource energy, large factories, and a great deal of specialization. The Industrial Revolution had begun.

(This is not to say that nothing at all was happening in the world for 60 or so centuries. There was, to be sure, great art, great literature and great music produced. But none of that altered the fact that it was still an agrarian world in which the main focus of nearly all human activity was food production—just getting enough to eat. And that took a lot of time and effort, because growing food was a real challenge. It was hard work.)

The second thing that happened was that at almost exactly the same time, in 1776, the United States was born, and that event, as much as or more than any strictly engineering, mechanical, or technical achievement, led to the advances that have made it possible for us to produce and enjoy the abundance we have today. With the free and voluntary economic arrangements that were possible in a unique way with the American political system as a base, people were able to use their individual talents to do as well for themselves as their efforts and their ideas and their courage to take risks would allow them to. What happened was that people simply were let alone to work and to strive. The result was the beginning of a prosperity and an improvement in the human condition—in basic living standards—the likes of which have not been matched anywhere else in the world at any time in history. And it was the kind of down-to-earth improvement that meant that working people were living measurably better in their day-to-day lives.

The fundamental freedoms that Americans had, that had been written and codified into our laws and had become a part of our way of life, allowed us to make maximum use, for our own personal good, of the new ideas that came along as the Industrial Revolution progressed. Those new methods were available to anyone in the world, but it was our system, here in America, that allowed us to benefit most from applying them, that offered the most motivation and the most personal incentive to get up and do things!

The history of the United States recounts the most rapid and broad-based improvement in the human condition in the history of the world. In fact, until the study of world civilizations progresses to the study of the United States, it is a consistent story of good living (but no more than relatively good) for the fortunate few and unrelenting hard work for the many. America changed that.

So where does that put us today?

Still different, still the same

No matter how much our methods of doing things may have changed over thousands of years of human history, our basic material needs and goals—providing ourselves with the food, clothing, and shelter we need to live—remain the same. The main change that can be observed is that instead of doing everything, or even most things, independently by ourselves and directly for ourselves, our lives now are built around interdependence and acquiring what we need indirectly with the help and cooperation of others, some of whom we'll never even see throughout our entire lives. The six basic principles still apply, of course, but in a more coordinated, organized, and productive way for us:

> Even though human life still requires human effort and we all still need food, clothing, and shelter, most of us don't acquire those things directly. We work for one person who employs us and obtain what we need from many other people who sell to us. What makes it possible for us to do that is that we use money.

> We still have to change what we find in nature into some useful, usable form, but we don't do the whole job from beginning to end ourselves or use directly the things we had a part in changing. What makes it possible for us to specialize that way and to divide the whole job up into many small bits and pieces and then trade back and forth easily is that we use money.

The basic function of any tool still is to convert energy into useful work, but instead of depending on tools that convert only muscular energy into work, we now use tools that convert the tremendous energy in natural resources into mechanical work. In addition, and of even greater importance to our living standards and our quality of life, we now use machines that do mental work for us. They are called computers. The reason that we are able to save enough to acquire and use so many tools is that we use money.

The freedom to hold private property still applies. But what we work for and strive for and earn and, therefore, may call our own today need not be what we usually think of as property at all. In fact, it is very easy for a person to own very little "property"—land, houses, and so on—and still be far from poor. Today, our security and peace of mind don't depend on having our own barns full of grain. What we rely on today are such things as savings accounts, mutual funds, pension or retirement funds, and insurance policies. What makes all of that possible is that we use money.

By now, you might have noticed a couple of things. First, much in our lives seems to depend on the existence and use of money. Money, of course, in one form or another, has been around for a long time. But it never has been as important in our daily lives as it is today. It never has been as necessary as it is now.

What we're talking about, however, is not just money in terms of paper currency or metal coins, and we're not talking about money in a miserly, greedy, and strictly materialistic sense. We're talking about money as a tool that does three very important jobs for us:

Money allows us to change our output, our human effort—no matter what we do for a living—into something we can trade to anyone else for what we need, no matter what that is.

18

Money gives us a means to measure the value of our effort, to determine what it is worth, and to compare it to the value of what we need so we can make the necessary exchanges.

Finally, money allows us to store up for the future, in a convenient form that doesn't spoil, the output that we've produced today but don't need to use today. It allows us to SAVE. And that's an extremely useful thing to be able to do. People can do a reasonable job of getting along from day-to-day by means of bartering and trading goods for goods, and goods for labor, and labor for labor, but any sort of genuine improvement in living conditions over the long haul requires the "saveability" that only money can provide.

Since the money we are paid as a wage represents the effort that we put forth on our jobs, it follows that the money we see all around us and use every day represents the total effort that is put forth by all working men and women throughout the entire economy. Later on, we'll look more closely at money and what it is and how it works. For now, it is enough to say that money represents human effort. It is someone's human effort that has given value, worth, and real purchasing power to all of those dollars and dimes we use every day. As tools go, money is the most useful, convenient, and powerful tool we have.

The other thing you might have noticed as we discussed how the six basic principles apply to our lives today is this: All the while that we've been talking about the way we live and work and provide for ourselves; and about the organizations and methods that we have developed and that we use to produce what we need to live; and about how living standards have improved steadily throughout history because of the use of tools, we haven't said a thing about government. And for a very good and simple reason.

Government institutions aren't a source of anything for us. Whatever we have in this world has been produced by working people. What any government agency or bureau or department spends on anything or anybody, it first must take from the only source there is—those individuals who have worked, produced something of value, and earned a wage. That is done, of course, by taxing people's earnings.

The only resources that any government has are taxes that are levied on what working people have produced.

That is not to say, however, that government institutions have no proper or useful functions, because they have. The primary one is to safeguard our most important right: The right to be let alone to go about the ordinary, day-to-day business of living and working and providing for ourselves and our families. That is what the Declaration of Independence is talking about when it says that we all have "…certain unalienable Rights, that among these are Life, Liberty, and the pursuit of Happiness. That to secure these rights, Governments are instituted among Men, deriving their just powers from the consent of the governed…."

Thomas Jefferson, the third president of the United States, spoke in his first inaugural address of "…a wise and frugal government, which shall restrain men from injuring one another, which shall leave them otherwise free to regulate their own pursuits of industry and improvement, and shall not take from the mouth of labor the bread it has earned."

When government protects the individual from harm and interference, from both foreign and domestic sources, when it protects property rights and enforces contracts, it creates a climate and set of living conditions in which people who want to can strive to do their best and to achieve all of the tremendous human good that we have achieved here in America.

But no government institution is a source of money or material goods. Only working men and women are.

Now that we've answered, in broad, general terms, the questions of how we live and where everything that we see around us has come from, the next step is to look at some of what we've talked about in more detail. In Chapter 3, we'll look at what makes the difference between just scratching out a bare existence, on the one hand, and being able to improve the way we live, on the other—our use of tools.

Capital makes a great difference in a person's day-to-day life. How much of a difference? The answer to that question can be discovered by looking at the way things are for people who don't accumulate and use capital and then looking at the way things are for people who do.

3 Capital

Just for a minute, try to imagine that never once throughout your entire life have you been able to sit down to a full meal and that you never will. In fact, you don't even know what eating a full meal is—that is, sitting down in front of a sufficient quantity of food, eating until you are full, and then getting up and doing something else.

But try to imagine also that the reason for that state of affairs has nothing to do with poverty or a low income as we understand and use those terms today. What then, other than a lack of money, could be the reason?

For a clue, you can look in some of the more remote areas of the world. To this day, there are some dozens of native tribes in Brazil, in the Amazon rain forest, who still have not advanced much beyond a Stone Age culture. They wander constantly in search of food. They have no industry; they don't build anything; and they don't trade with anyone. They don't have permanent homes or apartments the way we do or full-time jobs. Food gathering is about all they do. Something that is for us not much more than a weekly errand to the supermarket is their life's work. Why?

Because, for whatever the reason, they have not yet begun to make sufficient use of tools, not even the relatively simple tools needed to begin the most basic of all industries, agriculture. And without the tools that would enable them to produce and then store up more food than they require for their immediate needs, they simply haven't had enough time to stop worrying about feeding themselves and start doing other things that would give them what we in America have come to regard as a normal way of life: A home or apartment, indoor plumbing, central heating, basic appliances, an automobile, and so on.

The difference between those people and us is something called capital. We have it. They don't. Capital improves productivity. We have improved ours. They haven't improved theirs. As we have improved our productivity, we have seen our standard of living rise. Because their productivity never has improved, neither has their standard of living.

Now, you've just seen three common terms that are used every day but that still should be defined here because they often are thrown around carelessly:

Capital–In the broadest sense, the total of all of the tools—the equipment and buildings and land—that we use to multiply our limited human effort on our jobs. That term also is used to mean the money that must be saved or accumulated in order to acquire the actual physical tools we use.

Productivity–A measure of how much we can produce as a result of the effort we put forth. Obviously, when our productivity is high, we live better than when it is low. Raising our productivity, however, does not mean "back to the sweatshops." In fact, it means just the opposite: Using tools—capital —to pick up where human sweat leaves off. Nor does rising productivity mean fewer people producing the same total quantity of goods and services It means all of us together producing more for ourselves, more to have available here at home and more to sell in world markets.

Standard of living–How well we live in plain human terms, how well we can provide for ourselves and our families beyond the mere subsistence or survival level.

For most of the human race, tools, at least in some simple form, seem always to have been around, probably because making and using tools is almost a compulsion with us. Any time there is a job to be done, we reach for a tool. It's an extension of that basic human reflex to try to figure out a better way. And if there is no tool available, we devise one. In fact, one of the things we do better and more often than anything else in this world is to make tools.

Accumulating capital—saving out of current production to acquire tools—always has been the only way in which any material improvement in human life has been achieved.

In the United States, our capitalist economic system makes the process of tool acquiring and tool using serve the working man and woman better than any other system ever has at any time in history. And we have the results—our high standard of living —to prove it.

The way we do the actual acquiring and organizing of most of the tools we use is through private corporations. They are the voluntary arrangements mentioned in the last chapter. You will read more about them in the next chapter. For now, the following definition will do:

Corporations are voluntary organizations set up for the purpose of using saved money to acquire and organize the tools we all use on our jobs.

So how did we in this country develop into such great tool builders and users? As we already have seen, the increasing use of tools was a process that had been going on for thousands of years by the time Americans began to build on it. But although some progress was being made all along, the really big change has occurred over the last two centuries or so.

The way we were

The relationship between capital, productivity, and standard of living is almost a law of nature. However, the exact way in which they are related is no longer as obvious as it once was. To understand how the three are connected in our lives today, let's take a look back for a minute. But we don't have to go any farther back into history than the 1800s, and we don't even have to leave the United States.

In the 1800s, the United States still was primarily an agricultural country. In fact, the world at that time still was an agricultural world. Most people were farmers working their own land and providing themselves directly, as individual families, with the food, clothing, and shelter they needed. Yes, some things were purchased, but very few. There was manufacturing being done, and there were major cities, but what most Americans—about 97% of them—did to provide for themselves was to work their own land. The key thing is that they were producing most of what they needed by themselves directly for themselves.

At that time, our total accumulated capital, as a nation, had certain characteristics:

1. Capital was composed of tools that were personal items. People saved for and owned, as individuals, the things that helped them produce their food, clothing, and shelter. They owned the land (another tool) from which their food came.

2. Tools were relatively inexpensive.

3. Capital amounted mostly to tools that were simple devices: Hammers, axes, hand pumps for drawing water, hand-guided plows that were pulled by draft animals, hand looms, spinning wheels, and so on.

4. The benefits of the tools we used were direct and obvious, because we used them ourselves.

5. The payoff from the use of the capital that people employed was immediate. As soon as they had a mule pulling a plow, they could cultivate more land and grow more food than they could when they were using a hoe to cultivate by hand.

6. Most of the tools that were in the national capital stock in the 1800s converted muscular energy, either animal or human, into useful work for the tool user.

7. Overall, the purpose of the capital that people had was to help them attain the highest standard of living that they could for themselves and their families. It didn't make nearly as much difference what the rest of the country was doing. If others hadn't saved anything, it took nothing away from those who had. One person's standard of living didn't affect another's very much.

8. When it came to saving and accumulating the capital that an individual needed and depended on, government was a minor factor on a day-to-day basis.

If the average American family, therefore, wanted to live better, they knew what they had to do, and they were in a position to do it for themselves. They saved, or perhaps borrowed money; bought tools; and increased their productivity. In fact, there wasn't any other way for them to do it, or anyone else to do it for them.

But besides seeing right before them the need to save to buy new tools, people also could see the need for continued saving for two other reasons:

1. To replace the mule when it died and the plow when it wore out.

2. To buy improved tools even before existing tools wore out. Imagine how a farmer must have felt the first time he saw a new piece of agricultural machinery that would allow him to harvest, clean, and thresh all on the same pass through his fields. He didn't care that he had just bought a new single-purpose machine last year and that it was nowhere close to being worn out. He could see the advantages of the new machine and he wanted to start benefiting right away. By taking advantage of the newest and latest in capital equipment, a farmer could raise his productivity and achieve a higher standard of living for himself and his family.

Today, however, although the need to save and accumulate capital is less obvious, it is no less real. The tools that we use to increase our productivity, to raise our standard of living and improve our quality of life are in our factories and shops and offices, perhaps several miles away from our homes, instead of in our own fields and barns. We don't even see most of the tools from which we benefit. But the way in which those tools influence our lives is greater today than at any time in history.

27

Today, although tools and productivity still are important to each of us, we acquire the capital we need and produce the goods and services we need indirectly. Today, instead of doing the whole job alone, each of us does some small part, puts it together with the rest of the small parts that have been done by others, and together we all achieve our goal of providing for ourselves and our families. The reason has to do with the different kinds of tools we have and the different ways in which we use them:

1. The tools that we use on our jobs today are not tools that we have saved for personally and bought directly for ourselves. We do our saving and tool acquiring today as a nation. We save and accumulate our capital through banks and other financial institutions. We acquire our tools through corporations. In fact, the reason that corporations exist at all is to acquire and organize tools.

2. The amount of capital required today to put a single individual to work in a manufacturing job is well over $250,000. That would be quite a lot of money for one person to have to accumulate all alone. But what that means is not that things were so cheap in the past and are so expensive today. What it means is that today, because we use corporations to accumulate our savings and acquire our tools, one person can have a much greater amount of capital—tools—to use on the job than he could have working alone.

3. The tools that we use when we work today very often are not simple devices that perform simple tasks. Many of them are huge and complicated machines that do highly specialized jobs.

4. The way in which our total stock of tools helps us in our lives no longer is direct and obvious. In fact, we never see or even know about many of the tools that help us because we don't use them ourselves.

5. The payoff that we receive from the tools we use on our jobs is not immediate. It takes time to save the tremendous amount of money that our tools cost today. On the other hand, if we, as a country, aren't saving enough on a steady basis to provide ourselves with the tools we need, we'll feel the effects of the insufficient saving eventually. And given the rapid pace at which things change today, "eventually" very often is not that far in the future.

6. The energy that our tools convert today is not the small and limited energy in human or animal muscles, but the tremendous energy contained in natural resources.

7. Overall, the purpose of the capital we accumulate today is the same as the purpose of the capital that we had and used 200 years ago. Today, however, we succeed or fail together. If we don't generate the savings necessary to acquire the tools we need as a country, we all are in trouble together because our standard of living as a nation will start to decline.

8. In sharp contrast to the way things were in the early days of our country, government today, because of its spending, taxing, borrowing, and regulating policies, has a tremendous effect on how readily we are able to save and accumulate the money we need to purchase our tools.

TOOLS

In the 1800s	Today
Personal items, directly owned.	Owned by corporations.
Relatively inexpensive.	Very expensive--$250,000 per worker.
Simple devices for simple jobs.	Very complex systems that coordinate many separate steps.
Obvious benefits.	Benefit of a tool can be explained only as it contributes to improving a whole system.
Immediate payoff.	Tool acquiring often requires long lead times.
Converted muscular energy.	Convert natural resource energy.
Tool acquiring not dependent on what others did.	We now save, accumulate capital, and use tools as a country, and we succeed or fail together as a county.
Government a minor factor.	Because of its spending, taxing, borrowing, and regulating policies, government has a tremendous effect on how this country accumulates its savings and acquires new tools.

A good way to see the improvement that better and better tools have made in our daily lives over the past 200 years is to look around our own homes. Take today's modern homemaker. The jobs that need to be done around the house—cooking, cleaning, washing clothes—haven't changed, but the tools that are used to do them are vastly different, if indeed they existed at all in the 1800s. Gone are the wood stoves and washboards. In their places are electric and gas ranges and automatic washers and dryers. The same work still needs to be done, but the way it is done is very different. The same thing, of course, is true of yard work. It's a lot easier to do with power tools than it is by hand. Both indoors and outdoors, we see clear examples in our own homes of how tools increase our productivity and allow us to improve our standard of living

Financial intermediaries

We talked earlier about "banks and other financial institutions." We're all familiar with banks, but what are these "other financial institutions"? There are several different kinds and they all, including banks, are called "financial intermediaries." For all the fancy sound there is to the term, financial intermediaries are common, ordinary organizations that we see and use every day. We literally have grown up with them. They are the commercial banks in which we have our checking and savings accounts; the insurance companies to which we pay premiums (either we pay them directly or perhaps our employers pay them for us in our names); the pension funds to which we make contributions (again, either directly or through our employers); and the mutual funds into which we might put money to be invested in stocks and bonds.

What all of those organizations do is to take our money and invest it. How? One way is by allowing corporations to use it to acquire the tools we all use on our jobs. Another way is to loan it to consumers who want to buy homes and automobiles and washers and dryers. A third way is to loan money to the government by purchasing its securities. The return on that invested money comes back to the investing institution in the form of the interest and dividends that corporations pay; the interest that consumers pay; and the interest that the government pays. In that way, the financial intermediaries get the money they need to pay interest on savings accounts; to satisfy claims on insurance policies; and to make payments to participants in pension

Type of Intermediary	Source of Money	Primary Investment of Money	Use of Return on Investment
Commercial Bank	Deposits	Loans to consumers and businesses, purchases of government securities	Dividends to bank's shareholders, interest to depositors
Savings and Loan Institutions	Deposits	Mortgage loans, purchases of government securities	Interest to depositors
Insurance Companies	Premiums from policy holders	Stocks, bonds, purchase of government securities	Claims of policy holders
Mutual Funds	Sale of shares in the fund	Stocks, bonds, purchases of government securities	Dividends to fund participants
Pension Funds	Employer and/or employee contributions	Stocks, bonds, purchases of government securities	Payments to retirees

Who Gets What?

How are decisions made regarding who gets a loan and who is turned down? Individual savers, whether they are investing their savings directly themselves or indirectly through a financial intermediary, want to put their money where it will be safe and where it will earn them a return. That means either:

1. Investing it in a company that can pay dividends to shareholders and interest to bondholders, or

2. Loaning it (in the form of a mortgage, for example) to individuals whose income will allow them to return the

money they borrow (the principal) and pay for the use of it (the interest). Either way,

Interest is the cost of using purchasing power before you've actually saved it up yourself. It's the cost of credit. You are renting someone else's money.

Another fancy phrase we hear every so often is "capital allocation." That's what we're talking about here. In a free economy, individual savers, either directly or through their financial intermediaries, decide what is to be done with their savings, their capital, which stocks and bonds are to be purchased and who is to be given a loan. In a socialist economy, on the other hand, capital is allocated by the government. When savers make such decisions based on what consumers want, those who will be buying products in the marketplace control what is produced with limited saved money. The consumer is in charge.

Depreciation[1]

Depreciation, or "writing off" an asset, simply is a way of taking into account the fact that tools wear out and that, even before then, new and better tools are developed. (Recall the farmer a few pages back who had the one-year-old, single-purpose machine but who still wanted to buy the new and more productive combination machine he had just seen.) A corporation is permitted, logically, when it is calculating its taxable income, to subtract or deduct from its sales revenue the money that it must spend on wages, raw materials, utilities, supplies, and whatever else it buys to manufacture its product or provide its service. Such deductions affect a corporation's taxes the same way that deductions for mortgage interest payments or charitable contributions affect your personal income taxes: They reduce taxable income. Depreciation simply is a way that a corporation has of taking into account the fact that the usefulness of a

---

[1] The next three parts of this chapter--Depreciation, Accelerated Depreciation, and Investment Tax Credits—cover provisions in the federal tax codes that come and go. Sometimes they're on the books one way, sometimes another way, and sometimes they're not there at all. Actually, if there were no corporate income tax, there wouldn't be such things as allowances for depreciation or accelerated depreciation or investment tax credits, just as there would be no deductions for mortgage interest payments if there were no personal income tax.

piece of equipment decreases as time passes.   That happens for the two reasons already mentioned:

1. Things wear out. Shoes wear out. Tires wear out. So do tools and machines.

2. New and better machines are developed that make current ones obsolete.

But there is something different about the life of a machine, as opposed to the amount of electricity or raw material that is used in the course of manufacturing something, and that is this: Although you can calculate how much electricity was used to make a product, and you can see how much raw material was used, how do you figure out how much the usefulness of a machine decreased when the company made, say, 4,000 standard models and 3,500 deluxe models of its product? The only way to do it is to estimate what the useful life of the machine is and then spread out the decrease in usefulness as you manufacture the product. That allows you to treat the used-up life of the machine the way you treat the raw material and the electricity that you used: You deduct it as an expense that occurs during the manufacture of the product. It would look something like this on a company's books:

	With Allowance For Depreciation	Without Allowance For Depreciation
Sales	$99,000	$99,000
Less Cash Operating Expenses	-53,000	-53,000
Cash Provided by Operations before Income Taxes	46,000	46,000
Less Depreciation Expense	-10,000	NONE
Income before Income Taxes	36,000	46,000
Income Tax Expense (at 33.3% Rate)	12,000	15,330
Cash Provided by Operations before Income Taxes	46,000	46,000
Less Income Tax Expense (at 33.3 % Rate)	-12,000	-15,330
Leaves Cash Provided by Operations	34,000	30,670

Now what has just happened? From the $99,000 in sales income that the company has received from its customers, it has deducted as cash operating expenses $53,000 for such things as wages, raw materials, and utilities. That leaves $46,000, in cash, that has been provided by the company's operations. A year's depreciation, the reduction in usefulness of the company's tools, has been calculated to be $10,000. Deducting that amount leaves $36,000 in taxable income instead of $46,000, which was what taxable income was before depreciation. But look at this:

The $10,000 that was deducted for depreciation was a *non-cash* expense. It was not money that left the company the same as the money that was paid out to a utility or to a supplier of raw materials. The company still has $46,000 cash in hand. Taxes, therefore, if paid at a rate of 33.3%, will amount to $12,000 (33.3% x $36,000) instead of $15,330 (33.3% x $46,000.

A tax payment of course, *is* a cash outlay and is taken from the $46,000 in cash that has been provided by the company's operations, from its sales. With the allowance for depreciation, payment of taxes leaves the company with $34,000 in cash to use. Without that allowance, the company would be left with only $30,670 in cash to use. And how is any company going to use that money? To acquire and organize tools for its employees to use.

There are two other things that often come up in connection with depreciation and tool purchasing, and they are accelerated depreciation and investment tax credits.

Accelerated depreciation

In the example we just finished, all we talked about was the allowance for depreciation for one year. However, just about any tool lasts for a period of years. Let's say that the original cost of a machine is $41,000, that it is expected to last for four years, and that it finally will be disposed of for $1,000. Its depreciable value, then, is $40,000. If the method of straight line depreciation is used, the machine will be estimated to lose its usefulness evenly over its life at the rate of $10,000 per year for each of the four years.

With accelerated depreciation, however, the using up of the $40,000 worth of usefulness in the machine will be speeded up, for accounting purposes, in the early years of the life of the machine, leaving a smaller amount to be deducted each year towards the end. As an example, things might work out so that the depreciation expense is

$14,000 for the first year, $12,000 for the second, $8,000 for the third year, and $6,000 for the fourth and final year of the useful life of the machine. But the total still is $40,000.

Why accelerate the depreciation schedule? The advantage is that taking a bigger deduction sooner allows the company to get a hold of and use more of the cash produced by its operations just that much sooner. The overall effect is that the increase in the amount of cash available for use in the business will make it easier for a company to purchase newer, more productive, and more competitive tools for use by its employees. That's something that always has been important. Today, however, it's vital, because new technology and new and more productive machines are being developed so rapidly that if a company keeps just about anything until it wears out, competitors have a chance to get miles ahead with newer equipment. The company may never catch up, and it may never regain its competitive position. The almost sure result is permanently lost jobs.

Investment tax credits

The effect of an investment tax credit also is to make it easier for a company to purchase new and more productive equipment. If, for example, there is a 10% investment tax credit, and if a company invests $150,000 in new equipment during the year, the company may deduct 10% of that amount, $15,000 from the taxes it must pay. The company gets that 10% credit against its taxes because it has invested in new tools. It works like this:

Taxable Income	$300,000
Income Tax (at a 40% rate)	
Before Credit	120,000
Investment Tax Credit	-15,000
Income Tax Due	$105,000

The ability to save to acquire tools always has been necessary to improve the way we live. Today, however, it's very nearly a matter of survival. Competition, whether foreign or domestic, always is good. It keeps people and companies sharp. It gives a clear incentive to work hard, to find a better way. But when manufacturers in other countries can save for and acquire new tools more readily than American manufacturers can, we're at a disadvantage. When foreign manufacturers can give their employees better tools to work with than American manufacturers can provide for their employees to use, Americans are less productive, we're less competitive, and our products don't sell as well. That's how a country loses business. That's how manufacturing jobs are lost to overseas competitors.

All through this chapter, we've been talking about saving money and accumulating capital; about acquiring and organizing tools; and about how those tools help us. In Chapter 4, we'll take a closer look at the actual organization that does that acquiring and organizing—the corporation.

Using tools on an individual or a family basis makes possible a tremendous increase in productivity and living standards. But achieving the maximum benefit from the human ability to make and use tools requires that we pool our resources and capabilities. We must acquire and use tools on a large scale. And that is where corporations go to work for us.

4 The Corporation

Picture yourself in the following situation. Maybe you've already been there. If you have, God forbid it should happen again. But here you are, maybe you're married, and possibly there's a family. You have a home, a car, and all of the other normal and ordinary obligations that independent adult life in a free, democratic society involves. What you don't have at the moment, however, is a job. In fact, you've been out of work for about five months, and by now, you're feeling pretty depressed, pretty disgusted, and pretty sorry for yourself. You know what you can do for an employer and you're better than just OK at it. All you need is to connect with the right company.

Then one day at breakfast, you see a story in the morning paper about a medium-size company in town that is going to expand and do some substantial hiring. Applications will be taken starting today. At last your troubles are over, because one of the best openings they have is for someone with just your particular combination of experience and skills. Reading no further, you throw down the paper, shower, dress, and dash out the door.

Actually, you should have finished reading the article, because later on it says that anyone they hire has to put down a deposit of $250,000 to cover the cost of the machines and other capital equipment that the company is providing for its employees. It's something like a security deposit on an apartment: You get it back when you decide to leave, because the next person to come along will have to come up with it the same as you did. But still, you need that money now to get the job. Well, you don't happen to have $250,000 on hand, and by noon, you're feeling worse than you did when you sat down to breakfast.

The purpose of any corporation
is to acquire and organize capital, tools,
for us to use to generate an income.

Fortunately, however, it doesn't work that way in the real world, because finding the money and then acquiring and organizing the tremendous quantity of capital—tools—that we all use on our jobs every

41

day is done in this country mostly by corporations. What is a corporation? It's simply one of those voluntary arrangements that people form among themselves to get something done. It makes a product or performs a service in response to a consumer demand somewhere down the line.

Actually, the main function or purpose any corporation, no matter what it produces and offers for sale, is to acquire and organize capital. That provides the rest of us with the opportunity to use that capital and exchange our effort for an income.

But the really important thing to each of us personally is that a corporation allows us to be more productive by allowing us to use—per employee—a much greater quantity of tools than we ever would be able to save for and acquire on our own. In Chapter 3, we said that, on the average, over $250,000 worth of capital equipment is made available to each employee in the manufacturing sector. If, in order to provide for yourself, you had to come up with that much money in either tools or cash, could you do it? Or suppose that, in order to get a job, you had to put up $250,000 to cover the cost of the capital your employer would provide. Could you? Most people couldn't. In fact, hardly anyone could.

The life or existence of a corporation depends completely on the voluntary patronage of the consumer, whose demand for various goods and services is the reason that corporations are formed in the first place. No matter how big or how small it is, a private company has no source other than sales revenue for the income it needs to survive. Without that income from sales, it's in trouble. Period.

Some corporations are enormous, and a legitimate question is, Why? Why, for example, does General Electric Corporation employ over 300,000 people and ring up sales in one year (2013) of $146 billion? Why do the top 20 manufacturing firms in this country employ over eight million people and have combined sales in one year of over three trillion dollars?

The reason is that their size is a direct result of the size of the market they serve, and even if you consider only the domestic part of a company's market here in the United States, there are over 300 million of us in this country. What we need must be produced in tremendous quantities, and it would be prohibitively expensive to do it all by means of little, independent mom-and-pop businesses operating separately throughout the country. Only very large-scale acquiring and organizing of capital can produce what we need in the quantities we need and in such a way as to spread out the cost of production over enough products to make the price affordable.

> *A corporation allows us to use—per employee—*
> *more tools than we ever could acquire on our own.*

A thing that all corporations have in common, regardless of their current size, is that almost all of them started out very small with an idea and a few people (sometimes just one person) willing to risk money in the hope of achieving a payoff. Let's take a look at how such an enterprise might get going and then grow.

How it all begins

Let's say that you've come up with an idea for a new multi-purpose combination tool that would be extremely useful around the home. It's not going to revolutionize the world or alter the course of human history, but it's a nice handy little thing, and you're sure there's a market for it. You've talked to a few of your neighbors, and they agree that they could find dozens of uses for it around their homes and yards. So you're convinced! This thing is good, and you're not the only one who says so. Now what?

You figure that you probably can get started on a part-time basis. If you can get the right equipment, you can use half of your garage to make up a prototype model and get your device patented. Then you can take it around to the drug chains and discount houses to try to interest them in carrying it and maybe advertising it on TV and in the newspapers. But what you need right now to get going is capital, money that can be used to purchase equipment. You have your own savings of $6,000, but you figure that you'll need at least $4,000 more. You need an extra $4,000 of *venture,* or *risk, capital.*

A bank loan is pretty much out of the question. You haven't the collateral, and despite the fact that it's a good idea, you personally are an unknown quantity. The bank can't be sure that you have the business ability and the persistence to make even the best idea work. The bank, however, is able to give you a good suggestion. Instead of trying to raise all of the money in one lump sum from one source, why not try to get the money in smaller amounts from several sources. You could approach individuals by saying that, yes, there is a risk, but when this thing clicks with tens of thousands of consumers, you'll make some real money on your investment. And if, someday, stock in this new company is sold to the public, that could mean a really sizable gain for the original investors.

A corporation depends completely on the voluntary patronage of the consumer.

So that's what you decide to do. You'll offer some people you know a chance to buy a few small pieces of your new business and become owners with you. You are going to sell stock.

And here you are, setting yourself up in business the same as an automobile manufacturer or an oil company or a national appliance maker or any other major corporation. Different in size, of course, but the principles are exactly the same:

You are asking people to take a chance with you by putting up some of their   savings in the hope of getting a substantial reward for the risk they are taking.

You're going to be depending on the voluntary patronage of consumers for your sales and profits.

As big as an auto company is and as small as you are, if people don't buy their cars or your multipurpose tools, neither of you will have any revenue, you won't turn a profit, you won't stay in business, and you won't provide any jobs.

You manage to interest ten people in putting up $400 each by convincing them that it's a good idea to invest in your company. Furthermore, they can earn a return on their money without having to put any time or effort into the business. Their active participation is not required. You set the value of each share of stock at $10 and sell a total of

400 shares to your investors. That $4,000, together with your own $6,000, for which you'll receive 600 shares, gives you the $10,000 you need.

Off and running

So you get yourself started in your garage, and things are off to a great beginning. The tool is selling in the discount houses and the drug stores, and in about two years, you find that you've come to a point at which you have to make a tremendously important decision: Are you going to quit your job and go all the way with your product and whatever else may lie ahead, good, or bad? Or are you going to keep it just a part-time thing on a small scale? You decide to quit your job and go for it. But it's not going to be just more of the same. All those evenings and weekends that you've been working out in the garage, you've also been thinking about what else you might do, and by now, you have a few ideas sketched out. You don't want just to increase your production of multipurpose tools. You're going to expand and start producing the Towne & Country Line of Worksaver tools for home and yard.

But to do the job right, you're going to have to do more than just move out of your garage and into larger quarters. You'll need additional machinery—capital equipment—and some employees. Yes, you are at the point at which your business will be able to provide jobs for others. You're going to pay people to come in and use the tools that you've acquired and organized into a business. And that is success by any standard!

One quick and simple thing you can do to raise the money you need is to issue more stock. Considering that the business has been doing well and paying regular dividends all along, current shareholders would like to put a little more money into Towne & Country. Besides that, word of your success has got around, and there are a few more people who would like to invest in a young company that looks as though it has a good future. Because some of the original shareholders found themselves in need of ready cash in a hurry, there have been a few purchases and sales of your company's stock. In the process, the price has risen from $10 per share to $20 per share.

With your newly raised capital, you then line up a suitable building, do the required renovating, purchase the capital equipment you need (some of it used and not exactly what you want, but you'll make do for now), and run an ad for two employees. Your bank is able to put you on to someone who can handle your bookkeeping and accounting (all you need for now is a part-timer), and you're on your way on a much expanded level.

Nothing succeeds like success. It seems to feed on itself. Two more years whiz by. Your new line of Worksaver tools is really catching on, and you've been talking to a national retail chain about carrying your products. Those talks right now are still in the exploratory state, but there are two things on which you and the retail representative agree:

> Having the Towne & Country Worksaver line, now expanded to include a full assortment of garden and mechanics tools, carried by a national chain would be a tremendously good thing for both of you, but. . .

> Before the retailer can feel confident that you can produce in the volume that he will require, and before you can feel comfortable about promising to meet the chain's requirements, you both agree that you are going to need better production facilities. In other words, new plant and equipment.

You talk to your banker again, and you both come to the conclusion that the best way to raise the capital you need this time and for this purpose is to sell bonds. And that's what you do.

By now, you have sold stock twice—once to start your company and once again to expand—and you've sold bonds once to expand further. The stockholders are all owners of the company. The bondholders, on the other hand, are your creditors. The stockholders have purchased and now own a piece of the business. The bondholders have loaned you money. The stockholders will receive dividends when and if there are profits. The bondholders, as creditors, must be paid even if that means that there is nothing left over for the stockholders.

At this point, we've covered the basics of stocks (ownership of the company) and bonds (loans to the company). But we've done it for only one company and for only a tiny handful of shareholders. What about all the rest of the companies in the country and all of their shares of stock?

There probably isn't a single evening news program, local or national, radio or TV, that doesn't at least mention, however briefly, the stock market. And the number you get, even if you get nothing else, is what happened to the closing average of the Dow Jones 30 industrial stocks. Sometimes you don't even get the average; just how much it went up or down. "So what's it to me?" you might ask. "I don't own any stock. Why should I care what goes on in the market?" Before giving any answers, let's define a few commonly used terms:

Stock Exchange—A place where stocks, bonds, and other securities are bought and sold. The main one is the New York Stock Exchange.

The Dow Jones Industrial Average—This figure, or at least what has happened to it since the previous trading day, is what you get on the news. It is based on the prices of the shares of stock of 30 big, high-grade, "blue chip" U. S. industrial companies that are traded on the New York Stock Exchange. That figure is not by any means the entire New York Stock Exchange nor is it the entire stock market, but it gives a picture of what's going on with certain important stocks. Other "averages" that are figured and quoted each day are the Dow Jones average of 20 transportation stocks, the Dow Jones average of 15 utility stocks, the New York Stock Exchange Composite Index, and the Stand & Poor's 500 Index. But the average of the 30 industrials is the one that is most frequently quoted.

The Over-the-Counter Market—This isn't an actual place. It is an arrangement for bringing together buyers and sellers of shares of stock in small companies. Actively traded, over-the-counter (OTC) stocks are listed by computer. This is the NASDAQ (National Association of Securities Dealers Automated Quotations) system. The NASDAQ composite is another daily stock index that is followed widely. Until the company would meet certain requirements, mainly having to do with the size, number of shares of stock, and number of shareholders, Towne & Country shares would be traded—bought and sold—in the over-the-counter market, if the transactions weren't handled privately and directly between buyer and seller.

This now brings us to a very fundamental point about the stock market: What does it matter one way or the other what one share of stock is worth or what they're all worth?

The price of a share of stock, like the price of anything else in a free market, is based on what people think it is worth. The worth of a share of stock, in the end, depends on the profit potential—and, therefore, the dividend potential—of the company. In other words, how much are they going to give me if I let them use my money? How much money, how much profit will the company make by trying to sell its product or service? The answer to that question, then, will give an indication of how much profit there will be for direct saving to purchase tools and for dividends to attract the money of savers to purchase tools.

The health of the stock market is of interest because it gives an indication of the general health, the overall profit potential, of the U.S. economy. It gives an answer to the question, How able are the companies that we work for, and that produce what we need, to generate the necessary savings to acquire and organize tools and provide jobs for America's working men and women?

And where has all this taken us? Once again, we're talking about the same thing we talked about in the last chapter when we covered saving for the mule and the plow. Only this is what we do today to accumulate capital and acquire and organize the tools we need. For that reason, every American has an interest, and a vital interest at that, in the health of the stock market because of what it indicates: Our tool-acquiring ability as a nation.

The health of the stock market indicates our tool-acquiring capability as a nation.

What about the stock market as a place to invest for income? The effect of profits and stock prices and dividends on those who own shares of stock is obvious, and we've just covered why the stock market is important to the country in general. There are many people, however, who are not themselves direct shareholders, but who are affected nonetheless, and we touched on this in the last chapter. They depend on the stock market through such institutions as banks and pension funds and insurance companies (all of the financial intermediaries) to invest their savings to be able to pay them as savers, retirees, and holders of insurance policies. Because of what it represents—that is our basic tool-acquiring capability—what is happening on Wall Street to the stock market is of interest and importance to all American working men and women, and to their families, in one way or another. Not, to be sure, each and every little blip and ripple. It's the long term trend that matters:

> **If the stock market is going up over the long term** (after any necessary adjustment for inflation), we can look forward to a better life because the indication is that our employers can acquire more and better tools for us to use.

> **If the long-term trend is a flat line**, we shouldn't expect any meaningful improvement.

> **If the long-term trend is downward**, the indication is that we should expect to be less well-off in the future than we are today. Our tools will not be as good, and we'll be less productive and less competitive on our jobs.

Corporate taxes

Every so often you'll find someone saying on an evening news program or in the daily papers or somewhere that business should carry its fair share of the country's tax burden. And that sounds perfectly logical, of course, except for one thing: Businesses don't pay taxes. They simply transfer money from people to the government. Corporate taxes *always* are paid by people in the form of

> **Higher prices--**A tax, the same as any other cost a corporation incurs as it does business, must be covered in the price of the product. Ultimately, the consumer must cover all of the costs of any product, including the cost of the taxes that corporations must pay.

Lower wages--A single dollar can be spent only once. If it goes for taxes, it can't be used to pay wages

Reduced saving--But the thing that is affected to the greatest extent by taxes is saving for tools. Why? Think of what you would do. If you would happen to be a little short, you wouldn't be able to put off buying food, for example. You'd need that on a day-to-day basis. Maybe you wouldn't buy exactly what you'd want in exactly the amount you'd want, but you'd still buy food. The thing that would get shoved off into the future, though, is putting something in the family savings account. A corporation does the same thing. It has to pay for the necessities as it goes along, and although some economizing and cutting back is possible, wages still must be paid and materials and supplies still must be bought. What can and does get put off? Sufficient saving for tools. And insufficient saving for the tools we need to use on our jobs is what causes

> Declining productivity,
> Declining competitiveness,
> Declining standard of living, and
> Loss of jobs to overseas manufacturers.

Of course, there's nothing fundamentally wrong with paying some of our taxes directly to the government and passing the rest along through the corporations from which we buy what we need. The problem arises when we begin to believe that what business pays doesn't cost us anything. We can get something from the government for free because "business is picking up the tab."

When corporations pay taxes, they just transfer money from people—consumers, wage earners, and savers—to the government.

Capital gains tax

Earlier in this chapter, we talked about a small company that got started only because its owner was able to raise $4,000 in *venture capital*.

Supplying venture capital is a high-risk activity, because many new companies fail. The reason that it is done at all is that investors see an opportunity—not a guarantee, mind you; just an opportunity—to receive a substantial return on their money when the stock they own in a new and successful company eventually can be sold publicly at a higher price than they paid for it.

A capital gains tax simply is a tax on the increase in the value of an investment by the time it is sold. The greater the tax, of course, the smaller the net return to the investor, and the less incentive there is to risk money on a new venture.

Naturally, the supply of venture capital is like anything else: If you tax it, you'll get less of it. On the other hand, if you don't tax it, you'll get what people are willing to invest when they are free to make up their own minds about whether the risk involved in putting money into a new company is balanced by the potential payoff.

> *It is worthwhile to keep in mind that most new jobs in the American economy come into existence when new companies hire employees for the first time and when small and medium-size companies expand. Very large companies are not the principal job creators. The job opportunities are in the small and medium-size firms —provided that they can find capital to grow.*

We've just finished talking about how we acquire the necessary tools to produce the goods and services we consume from day to day: By means of the private corporation. In Chapter 5, we'll talk more about how a corporation obtains money to acquire those tools and how the consumer controls their use.

It hasn't been possible to discuss profit until now because the real explanation of profit lies in

>The way working men and women live and provide for themselves   (Chapter 2);

>The fact that we need to use tools if we are to work—and therefore to live—better (Chapter 3); and

>The way in which we save to acquire and organize the tools we need (Chapters 3 and 4).

>In other words, the only way to explain profit is in terms of how it serves individuals   as producers of what they need and as consumers of what they produce.

>*Profit is what ensures that the real economic decisions in America are made not in corporate boardrooms or in government offices, but in the aisles of this country's supermarkets, along the counters of its department stores, in the showrooms of its automobile dealerships, and in all the other places in which working Americans spend their money.*

5 Profit

Which of the following statements are true, and which are false?

1. The purpose of any business organization is to produce a profit.

2. There is no such thing as profit.

3. The purpose of any business organization is to produce a flow of cash.

4. Every organization—regardless of whether it is run by capitalists, communists, socialists, Marxists, the clergy, or the U.S. government—must strive for, produce, and then use profits, at least in some form, regardless of what the money is called.

Actually, they're all true, including the second one and the last one. To help explain why they all are true, however, it's necessary to define "profit" and examine its uses.

Profit is what is left over from the total revenue taken in by an organization after all current expenses and costs—wages, raw materials, office supplies, and all the rest—have been covered. You are taking in more than you are spending as you operate from day-to-day.

We all like a profitable operation when we benefit from it reasonably directly and can see how that is happening. For yourself, you like it when your income is greater than your expenses. As an individual, you are a "profitable operation." And when employers are profitable, because the income they get from the sale of their products is greater than their expenses, individuals benefit personally because their jobs are more secure. If an employer is growing and expanding and prospering, there might even be better jobs and more money for employees. (Of course the opposite also is true: When a business does not do well, neither do its employees.)

But what about all those other companies out there? Sure, it's nice to have everyone working, but do the profits of employers in general have any effect on the individual, one way or another? What about all those profits that "Big Business" is making?

Money that does things

Nothing exists without some good reason, and the only reason profits exist is to satisfy a need. If that weren't the case, then simply breaking even from day-to-day would be enough.

Profits serve three purposes:

1. **Profits are a saving device that we use to acquire the tools we need.**

There are only two things that a corporation can do with its profits:

--It can keep them and save them. Such direct savings are called "retained earnings."

--It can pay them out as a return to the owners, the people who have purchased   shares of stock in the corporation and thus given it the use of their savings. Such payments are called "dividends." (Interest payments to bondholders, on the other hand, are a current business expense, along with wages and materials.)

Dividend payments are made in two ways:

--Directly to individuals who are shareholders of the company.

--Indirectly to individuals who have put their money into financial intermediaries (banks, insurance companies, mutual funds, and pension funds), which then have used those savings to purchase, among other things, shares of stock. But one way or another, dividends always wind up, in the end, going to individuals who have saved and then somehow invested—risked—their money.

2. Profits are a communication device.

Because profit is absolutely essential to the survival of any private organization, it works as a means of communication as well. It is a signal to those who are running the business: If there is enough profit to keep the organization going, it means that consumers feel they are getting value for their money when they purchase that company's product. They are willing to cover the whole cost of producing it, including the cost of the necessary tools. If, however, consumers, as a group, don't feel that a good or a service gives them value for their money, there won't be sufficient sales and there won't be sufficient profit. And sooner or later, that product won't be on the market, because the manufacturer will have to take the hint and stop using his limited resources to make it. And that's OK.

It's not greed that determines where saved capital will go and what sort of business it will be used to finance. It's consumer approval or disapproval.

3. Because the message that consumers send can't be ignored, profits are a means of control.

There is no communication just because one party is talking. (Parents claim that they notice this at times when they are talking to their children. Children, for their part, say that they notice the same thing occasionally when they are talking to their parents.) In fact, even having a means of transmitting information doesn't guarantee successful communication. Not only must there be a sender of information and a means of transmitting it, there also must be someone on the other end who is listening and who *must* pay attention. Without a producer who is forced to depend on profit for survival, the consumer—the payer of the costs of production—has no voice. And to carry one step further the idea that having to depend on profit requires producers to be good listeners, it is the *expectation* of profits, which

will come only with consumer approval, that provides the
incentive for people to risk their savings and bring forth
new products for sale.

Now, as promised in Chapter 1, here is the story of the Edsel and
the Mustang. It's short, but telling. Few, if any, products ever have been
brought to market with as much ballyhoo and good old American hoopla
as the 1958 Edsel. If someone had said that Ford Motor Company spent
more money on advance publicity for that one car that they did on the
tooling to manufacture it, who could argue? To cut a short product life
down to an even shorter story, after two highly disappointing model years
in 1958 and 1959, production of the 1960 Edsels, which would have begun
around September of 1959, was halted in November.

And the Mustang? When it was introduced scarcely four years
later, it became, from the moment of its birth, a legend that lives to this
day. Unable to move the Edsel despite its best efforts, Ford could barely
keep up with the demand for the Mustang. And it was the same company
in the same industry in the same country offering the same type of product
to the same pool of potential buyers. What made the difference? Nothing
other than the freedom of choice that consumers in a free-market capitalist
economy have. To buy or not to buy? That was the question. And the
people answered in such a way that they could not be ignored.

And it was all a matter of profit, the ultimate, the final consumer
hotline.

Now we can go back to the four statements at the beginning of this
chapter and see why they're all true.

1. **The purpose of any business organization is to
   produce a profit.** This does not indicate a shameful
   "lust for gold" on the part of a bunch of greedy business
   executives. It's just a simple statement of fact. Just as
   the purpose of a cell phone is to provide a means of
   communication, the purpose of a corporation, the
   reason it is set up by individuals in the first place, is to
   acquire and organize tools. To acquire tools, of course,

requires savings, which come from profits. What it amounts to is this:

A corporation is a voluntary arrangement or organization set up to acquire tools.

Both saving directly and obtaining and paying for the use of the savings of others is possible only if there is something left over after immediate, day-to-day expenses have been covered. Those "leftovers" are called a company's profits.

2. **There is no such thing as profit.** This isn't just playing tricks with words. Profit very often is talked about and written about in the media as if it were excess money that isn't needed for anything and can be restricted without ill effects. And, in that sense, it doesn't exist—for a corporation. Corporate profit is money that fills a definite need in our lives: *It covers the cost of the tools we all use on our jobs.* That's obvious as far as retained earnings are concerned, but it's just as true for dividends. Dividends, once they have been paid out to shareholders for the use of their savings, then might be spent by those shareholders on leisure items. But to a corporation, dividends are the price that must be paid for the use of the savings of individuals, the price of persuading them to risk their savings.

3. **The purpose of any business organization is to produce a flow of cash.** This is a relatively modern way of looking at how a business operates, and it takes us back to something we mentioned in Chapter 3, Capital: One thing that employees and employers have in common is that they both need to have someone to part with money and give it to them. They both need cash to cover their expenses so they can survive. The employee calls it earning a wage. A corporation calls the process "generating a flow of cash." It's the old

familiar story about nothing happening until someone does something. In this case, no profits are produced, no money is saved, no tools can be acquired, and no jobs are provided unless money changes hands from consumer to producer.

4. **Every organization—regardless of whether it is run by capitalists, communists, socialists, Marxists, the clergy, or the U.S. government—must strive for, produce, and then use profits.** The idea that income must exceed day-to-day expenses applies not only to businesses but to charitable institutions, churches, social clubs, fraternal organizations, individuals, and anything else in this world. If you are going to stay alive and continue in operation, you need that little bit extra, that little bit left over.

To expand a bit on the fourth point, recall again that the purpose of profit is to produce—both directly and indirectly—saveable money to acquire tools. And, no matter who owns a piece of equipment, no matter what kind of political or economic system a country has, that piece of equipment has a useful life of only so long before it is worn out. The initial acquiring of tools and their replacement requires saved money— period. We capitalists call that saveable money "profit." Communists would call it "surplus." But whatever you call it, it amounts to the same thing, and it's necessary in order to acquire tools.

The money that is needed to construct and maintain the buildings and other physical equipment of a religious organization, a fraternal group, a social club, or any other nonprofit group does the same job. And the same thing is true for any government operation. Government ownership does not eliminate the need to produce money in excess of current expenses. The U.S. Postal Service, for example, during an average year, doesn't even cover its day-to-day expenses from its revenues, much less produce any leftovers. The reason that it keeps going, however, is that it still gets the "profits" it needs in the form of a subsidy from general federal tax revenues.

However, though the need for "profit" is still present, something else is absent from a situation involving a government organization, and that is the second party on the other end of the consumer hotline who *must* listen and then respond *promptly* to the consumer in order to survive. A steady supply of tax revenue and the essentially unlimited borrowing power of the government means that there is no need for any federal agency—here or in any other country—to move very fast to please the consumer, because the continuous, voluntary patronage of the consumer isn't needed for survival.

No matter how you look at it, profit does three things.

1. It gives us the tools that we need to earn a living.

2. It tells a corporation what it must do with those tools in order to satisfy the consumer, stay in business, and provide jobs.

3. It gives consumers ultimate, final control over what a private company puts on the market.

In all cases, profit operates to the advantage of working Americans, both as producers and as consumers.

How big?

Every so often, a newspaper or a TV network or somebody else will put up some money to sponsor a poll to find out what Americans are thinking about one thing or another. Whenever the subject of the poll is corporate profits, two questions always are asked.

How big do you think corporate profits are as a percent of sales?

How big do you think a fair profit is for a corporation as a percent of sales?

The answer to the first question usually averages out to be about 25%. The answer to the second question usually averages out to be about

10%. The correct figure is about 4.5%. (In the retail grocery business, the figure is even lower—about 1.5% or so.) But the interesting thing is that none of those numbers means anything. In a free market--that is, in a situation in which consumers are free to spend or not to spend with a certain producer, and in which producers are free to enter or not to enter a line of business--profits are governed by two things: (1) The desire of consumers to have a certain product, and (2) The freedom of multiple producers to supply it.

1. If consumers want a particular product or service, they will be willing to pay a price that not only will cover the day-to-day operating expenses of the producer but that also will cover the cost of the tools needed to make that item or provide that service. But that only puts a floor under profits and keeps them at a minimum level. What keeps them from going up without any limit? That is the second thing in a free economy that governs the size of a company's profits.

2.   Profits in a free market will rise until they begin to attract other producers, who see that consumers are willing to pay a price that allows a profit, and who want to get in on the action. The competition for the business of the consumer, who may buy from whomever he wishes and naturally prefers to pay the lowest possible price, keeps profits and prices from going up without any limit. In fact, prices in a free market will tend to come down due to increased competition. For example,

Automobiles once were luxury items, but as more producers entered the business and found better and less costly production and marketing methods, prices fell so that now automobiles are an everyday item.

Television sets, which at first cost nearly as much as a new automobile and had only tiny, round, black-and-white screens, now are available with huge screens that produce color pictures. And the price of a television set today is only a fraction of the price of an automobile, and quality has improved tremendously.

Hand-held calculators, when they first came out in the 1960s or so, cost over $100. Today that capability is a mere app on a device that puts the world in the palm of your hand.

Profit is the consumer's voice and producer's ears. The way in which Americans buy their food provides another clear example.

Fast changes in fast food

Eating in restaurants to the extent that we do is a definite break with tradition that began only about 30 or 40 years ago. That change in eating habits, moreover, occurred very rapidly. In just one ten-year period, the number of total food dollars that Americans spent in restaurants and fast food shops rose from one dollar in five to one dollar in three. (The balance was spent in grocery stores.) That was an increase of over 50% in the amount of money we spent eating out compared to what we spent eating at home. That's a substantial change.

The reason that consumers were able to make the change and do it so rapidly was that producers not only saw the opportunity to earn a profit on the changing eating habits of Americans, they were free to respond to that change and to do it rapidly. And the competition for the consumer's dollars in the fast food business is fierce. The result has been that the opportunity for many producers to compete freely for the consumer's dollar makes it impossible for any single producer to charge whatever he likes.

That opportunity also has meant that there is a lot more available to the consumer than just hamburgers. Originally, there was only one truly national fast food chain. Today, there are dozens. In addition, hungry consumers now can get much more than just hamburgers under a couple of golden arches. When they want a change, they can go into little huts and get pizza. Or they can purchase seafood from a well-known one-legged sea captain. Or they can head south of the border.

Also, what started out as a limited selection of burgers, fries, and soft drinks now is a huge catalog of superburgers and sandwiches of chicken, fish, ham, roast beef, cold cuts, and almost any other kind of food that will fit between the two halves of some sort of bread product. And there is breakfast fare as well. And of course the availability of dinner salads in virtually every restaurant in the country, in response to consumer demand for lighter foods, is another free-market phenomenon.

The opportunity that is available to all would-be producers to earn a reward, a profit, by competing successfully for the consumer's business has brought forth this huge number of producers. At the same time, the great number of choices available to the consumer has made it impossible for any one of those producers to charge a higher-than-competitive price.

The fast food industry is, of course, just one example. Exactly the same thing is true with automobiles, appliances, or anything else in this free-market economy of ours.

What's done, what's ahead

So far in this book, we've examined generally how people live, what tools are, and how we acquire and organize them. We've also learned how consumers in a free society control the way in which limited resources are used and determine what products are made. With that as background, we're now ready to begin dealing with something that, when it is not a fact of life in the present, is always a threat to us in the future—inflation.

By way of laying the necessary ground work, we next will discuss money, and then we'll examine banks. Finally we'll be ready for the main event, Chapter 8, Inflation.

Human progress always has depended on understanding the effective and proper use of tools to make our efforts more productive and indeed to make it possible for us to do some things that we could not do at all without tools. Today, we depend on a greater variety of tools than at any other time in history. But curiously enough, the one tool that we depend on most is not some mechanical device or even a modern computer. It is money. Using something—anything—for money is a tremendously useful and convenient arrangement for us. Our lives would become very difficult if all of a sudden we had to start trading and bartering for everything we need.

But the use of money is a mixed blessing, because if it were not for the fact that we use something for money, we would not, could not, have inflation. If we were paid, at the end of our work week, in bread and meat—so many loaves of bread and so many pounds of meat for our 40 hours of work—the cost of our groceries would never go up. The unavoidable fact is that the use of money puts something, over which someone else has control, between us and the things we want to buy. As a result, the potential for inflation exists. Occasionally that potential is realized.

6 Money

Suppose that you were to wake up one morning, look out your window, and find the ground covered with money. In every yard and field and street around you. As far as the eye could see, there are fives, tens, twenties, fifties, even hundreds. All over the place. More than likely, after recovering from the initial shock, you'd rush outside with a bag or a box and begin scooping up as much as you could. Maybe you'd use a leaf rake and put it all into a giant plastic trash bag. You'd look around, and you'd see your neighbors doing the same thing. Everyone laughing and shouting, waving and calling back and forth about what each of them will buy first.

The more you gather up, the faster your mind races along as you make up your own shopping list. There's plenty in the bag now to pay cash for a new car or two or three. And a plane would be nice. A small jet. Another three or four bags (depending on how many hundreds you find), and you'll have enough for a beachfront home. After all, sun is good for you. In fact, the sun on the French Riviera might be even better. Yes, a European vacation definitely is called for. And so the list goes on. Sounds like heaven, doesn't it? Well it wouldn't be.

Not worth the paper it's printed on

What it would be is the beginning of the worst kind of agony that you could imagine, because none of that money would be worth anything. Not only would you not be able to use any of your new-found "wealth" to pay cash for the car or the beachfront home or the vacation or any of the rest of it, you wouldn't even be able to buy a pizza. Or a T-shirt. Or a used CD. Or a fun-size candy bar.

Why not? Because who would sell you anything of value for mere money? Why give up something useful for some kind of a piece of paper you can find lying around the back yard? And that wouldn't be the worst of it. Any savings that you might have accumulated would be worthless, too. In short, all money would be worthless, no matter how hard you or anyone else had worked for it.

In a sense, however, that wouldn't make any difference, because in about a week or so, there wouldn't be anything to buy. Nothing would be produced because people wouldn't work. Why should they? Who would be willing to put in a full 40-hour week only to wind up with a few pieces of paper the same as the ones that are lying around in the streets? It would be like paying a person off at the end of the week with a bag of grass clippings.

How could anyone survive under such circumstances? You might be able to do yourself a little bit of good *if*, for example, you had just purchased some new clothes, and *if* you were able to find a grocer who took your size, and *if* the grocer also happened to like the style and color of your clothes. In that case, you might be lucky enough to be able to trade your clothes for perhaps a week's worth of groceries. But that's an awful lot of *"ifs."* And then what about next week?

Overall, it doesn't take a lot of heavy analysis to figure out that the chances are very good that the entire economy would grind to a halt very quickly. No one would work. No one would produce anything. There would be, to put it mildly, intense competition for anything useful. People would try to grab anything of value that might help them survive. In fact, people would just be grabbing whatever they could lay their hands on, regardless of whether it would be of any real use to them. Looters would be a menace everywhere.

Actually, you could bet a year's pay (not that that would mean anything) that there would be not only looting, but chaos and a general breakdown in law, order, and normal life. And all this would occur, in all probability, in less than a week after the appearance of all that new money. The only course of action that would have a chance of getting the country back on its feet and preventing total, permanent collapse of the entire economy and the entire country would be the suspension of individual freedom and the imposition of martial law. What shocks and angers the entire free world when it takes place in a repressive dictatorship would have taken place in America.

And what would have happened? Something that most people would call a purely economic event—the sudden appearance of a lot of money—would have resulted in the disappearance or, at the very least, the indefinite suspension of our basic political liberties and human freedoms. (Recall what George Marshall and Milton Friedman said back in the Introduction.) Because our money would have become worthless, we would have ceased to be a free people. Far-fetched? Silly? Impossible? In one sense, yes. In another sense, absolutely not.

Yes, because it is indeed highly unlikely that you will wake up one morning and discover that during the night someone has flown over the country and dumped money from a plane. But the thing that is not far-fetched is the idea that there is a direct connection between the amount or quantity of money in this country, relative to what there is to buy, and your ability to live as a free person. The reason for this is that there is a direct connection between the amount or quantity of money in any economy and the worth or value of each individual dollar that you earn and then either save or spend.

Of course the value of your money doesn't have to go to zero overnight, as happened in the example. It doesn't even have to go to zero. It can diminish gradually and steadily over a period of years.   But the result is the same. When the total quantity of money in circulation increases, relative to what there is to buy, the value of each of your dollars decreases. And as the value of your money decreases, your ability to purchase what you want and to live as you want decreases. Which explains why, if you want to control people, all you need to do is figure out a way to control the value of their money. Consider this true story:

> During World War II, those who ran the Nazi war machine earned the reputation of being not just ruthless but cunning as well. They knew that any country depends for its military strength both on a solid economic base at home and on its ability to buy goods from other countries. Destroy, even weaken, that base at home and that purchasing capability abroad, and the war was a long way toward being won.

> To succeed against England, the Nazis devised a plan to undermine the British economy, and in so doing, severely limit that country's ability to produce and purchase what it needed to defend itself. The idea was

67

simple: Flood England and the neutral countries with counterfeit English currency.

By 1945, the Nazis had succeeded in producing counterfeit British currency worth the equivalent of nearly half a billion American dollars. It was so good that it was passed both by Swiss banks and by the Bank of England. Fortunately, however, even though it was used to some extent, the war was ended militarily by the Allies before the counterfeit money was able to achieve its maximum destruction. But the idea of destroying a country by destroying the value of its money was, and still is, completely valid.[2]

Voting with ballots, voting with dollars

We Americans are very conscious and very aware of the idea of political freedom. It's our political system, really, that distinguishes us from the rest of the world, and there are a number of ways in which we exercise our political freedom. Few people would dispute, however, that one of the most visible ways that we do that is by voting. We vote to pick our leaders. We vote on issues. And when we go to the polls, it's for a real election, not just to give rubber-stamp approval to something a military dictatorship already has decided. Even the person who doesn't vote at all would find it difficult to deny that our free elections are probably the most important and obvious symbol of our overall political freedom and that they *do* make a difference. And of course the thing that affects the outcome of all of our elections is the sum of all the votes, all of the individual decisions, of all of the people who cast their ballots.

But suppose that someone were to come along and say to you that gradually—little-by- little, day-by-day, year-by-year—the power of your vote in presidential and congressional elections (to look at things just at the federal level) would be cut in half over a period of seven years. The other half of your vote would be taken by the government and given to

---

[2] A book on this very interesting piece of history was written by Anthony Pirie. Published in 1963, it was called *Operation Bernhard.* A more lighthearted account of the same historical events ran as a multi-part series on public television in 1984 under the title "Private Schultz."

some federal agency or to some other individual to cast as that person would see fit. You simply wouldn't stand for it. If you wouldn't hold still for that, then consider this: When the rate of increase in the cost of living is running at, say, 13.5%, the purchasing power of your dollar ballot, every time you buy something and "vote" at a cash register, will be cut in half in less than seven years. In 1979, not that terribly far back, the annual rate of increase in the cost of living was 13.5%. The value of the dollar was declining that rapidly a mere three and a half decades ago.

There is no point in spending a lot of time explaining how rising prices hurt you, but a couple of things should be said:

1. As already explained, above and in the last chapter on profit, every time you buy something, you vote with your money. You tell the producer of some product or service, "I like this stuff. Keep it coming." You tell the rest of the producers that you don't like what they're offering quite as well. That's how you, in a free-market economy, control what appears for sale and control the way in which limited production and manufacturing resources are put to use.

2. Monetary soundness and stability are so closely tied to your day-to-day individual freedom, and vice versa, that it simply isn't possible to have one without the other.

A very useful tool

In the chapters that dealt with the way we live and with capital and tools, we said that tools are devices that we develop to help us get our work done more easily and efficiently so we can be more productive for ourselves. The same is true of money. It also is a tool. It is the most important and useful tool ever developed, and it does three important jobs for us:

1. It allows us to change our output, no matter what we do, into something we can trade to anyone else for

whatever we need, no matter what that might be. It's completely versatile.

2. It allows us to measure the value of our output and to put a value on what we need so we can make the necessary exchanges.

3. It allows us to store up for the future, in a convenient and durable form, what we've produced today but don't need to use today.

And when it comes to improving our standard of living, the third thing that money does for us—allowing us to store our current but unneeded output, allowing us to save—is by far the most important. Even though bartering or trading is slow and inefficient, it still can be done, and people can survive that way, although not very conveniently, on a day-to-day basis. But there are very few commodities that are as "storable" as we need them to be, as "storable" as money is. Other things either spoil or they take up too much room or they can't be moved around easily or something else is wrong with them. What it all boils down to is that to do the saving that we need to do, we need money.

Recall that we said in Chapter 3, Capital, that human beings always have been natural toolmakers; that if they saw a job that needed to be done and there was no tool around to do it, they'd invent one; and that the making of tools probably is one of the jobs that humans do best. The same thing applies to the tool we call money. Throughout the whole history of the world, whenever there was a need for money but there was no money around, people would invent it. And when what they had invented, usually coins and paper money, was taken away from them, they'd agree on something else. It's almost a reflex, an instinct.

One example of this is the use of cigarettes as money in penitentiaries and prisoner-of-war camps. Smokers and nonsmokers alike. It made no difference. Everyone used them. The way in which cigarettes have been used successfully as a workable, useful kind of money also tells us a couple of very interesting and very fundamental things about our own money, both metal and paper.

For one thing, in order to do the job we want it to do for us, whatever we use for money need not have any value in and of itself. The reason for money's great usefulness—and the reason that sellers will accept it from buyers—is that the sellers know that they, in turn, can exchange it for what they want. Look at the nonsmoker in the POW camp. To him, cigarettes—as cigarettes—were of no use at all. But they still were valuable to him because he could exchange them for other things that he did want.

And the same is true of our money today, both coin and currency. A dime does not contain a dime's worth of metal, and a $10 bill certainly is not made of ten dollar's worth of paper and ink. But both are useful to us because of what they represent—purchasing power. We can trade them to someone else for something we want that is of use and value to us. The second person accepts our money and gives us his product or service because he knows that he, in turn, can trade or "spend" that same money for something he wants, and so on down the line. We acquire our money in the first place by trading our labor, our effort, for dollars that we then use to obtain what we want.

The second thing that the use of cigarettes for money tells us is this: The value of an individual piece of money, whether it is a cigarette or a dollar bill, depends on and varies with the number of other pieces of money in circulation, relative to what there is to buy. In the POW camp, a sudden increase in the supply of cigarettes would cause the prices of everything, figured in terms of cigarettes, to go up. The value of an individual cigarette, of course, would go down.

Not even the value of gold, whether in the form of minted coins or pure nuggets, can remain unaffected by an increase in its quantity. Two examples of that occurred during the famous gold strikes in California and Alaska. The sudden and very large increase in the quantity of gold in all the small mining towns, even in the form of dust and nuggets, resulted in such things as $5 price tags on ordinary chicken eggs. And this was $5 about 175 years ago in the middle of the nineteenth century!

In the sixteenth century, when gold and silver coins were the typical hand-to-hand money, there was inflation in Europe because of all the gold and silver that Spain was bringing back from Mexico and South America.

Money is a tool, and just like any other tool that you use at work or around the house, it can be a great help if it is used properly and for the purpose for which it was intended. If, however, it is used improperly, a tremendous amount of harm can be done with it. More about that in the next two chapters.

Money is a tool that represents human effort. We obtain it by working at something that someone else will pay to have done. It is a tool that does three important jobs for us: It enables us to exchange, to measure, and to save our effort. Money is, in short, a good, useful, and necessary thing. But a bank can do something with money that we can't do. A bank can create it, and that's a good, useful, and necessary thing, too. It's done every single day. In fact, if it weren't done, our human progress wouldn't be nearly what it is today.

7 Banks

Some people have been performing, and the rest of us have been using, some of the services of today's modern banks for thousands of years. Indeed, banking has been around ever since there has been money. Even before the time of the ancient Greeks, such basic banking services as lending, exchanging one kind of currency for another, and the safekeeping of money were available. But even though there was money and some form of banking, there still was a good deal of barter and trading of goods for goods, goods for services, and services for services. (That kind of thing still goes on today, of course, but most often, it is the exception rather than the rule, as you know from your own daily experience.) And that's the way things were until about the 1600's in Europe.

The real forerunners to today's modern banks were the goldsmiths. People who had more money on hand in the form of gold or silver coins than they needed at the moment would leave it with a goldsmith for safekeeping and pay him to hold it for them. The goldsmith gave the depositor a receipt. That receipt was safe and, of course, much more convenient to carry around than a chest full of gold or silver coins.

But people discovered that the goldsmith's receipt had another advantage. Instead of going to the goldsmith to draw out coins to pay debts and make purchases, they simply could pass the receipt along to creditors and merchants. By using them in this way, people had converted the goldsmith's receipts into the first hand-to-hand paper money.

Another practice that became popular was the writing of letters by depositors to the goldsmiths, directing them to pay out money from the depositor's account to someone else. By writing such a letter, a person at that time could accomplish exactly what we accomplish today when we write a check. By means of a check, we tell our bank to give money that we have on deposit to someone else. And of course it's the same thing with debit cards.

Now, while the public was discovering this system of currency and checks, the goldsmiths were making a few discoveries of their own. One thing that they noticed was that when depositors, as a group, put money into the goldsmith's vault or strongbox for safekeeping, some of that money just stayed there. There were withdrawals, and there were deposits, of course, but when you matched the two together, it worked out that most of the time they just canceled each other out, and a certain amount of money always stayed in the vault. So why not generate a little income by loaning some of it out? The practice of making loans worked so well that the goldsmiths no longer just sat back and waited for people to leave their gold and silver coins with them. They began to go out and look for depositors and to offer to pay them money—interest, in other words—to leave their gold and silver coins with them.

Another discovery that the goldsmiths made was that because their receipts were being used as money, they, in turn, could make their loans by giving borrowers their promises to pay gold coins instead of actually giving borrowers the gold coins. They also discovered that they could give out more of those promises to pay than the actual amount of coins that people had on deposit with them. But so much for history. Let's move up to our own times and activities.

Banking today

Ever since there has been money, no matter what form it has been in, there has been a demand for it. Indeed, the reason money was devised or invented in the first place was to fill a need in the day-to-day affairs of people. What's more, there always has been a demand by people for more money than they have had on hand. In other words, there always has been a demand for lendable funds.

And why not? Money is a useful tool. It performs a service for us that we need. And the greater use we make of tools, the better off we are. Consumers, for example, need to borrow money to buy furniture and automobiles and hundreds of other things that they want now but for which they don't have the necessary savings on hand. Businesses also need to borrow money to purchase tools both for replacement and for growth. They need to finance inventories so that production runs smoothly and so that customers can buy products from the shelf instead of having to wait for them to be made. Businesses also borrow to meet their employees' payrolls until customers pay for what they have bought on credit.

76

The principle is the same

There are two kinds of organizations today that we call banks:

Savings and loan institutions

Commercial banks

With all of the different and expanded services and conveniences that all banks are offering these days, the difference between the two types is not as great as it once was. Basically, however, you still can say that the savings and loan institutions simply take money in through one window from savers and loan it out to borrowers through another window. Generally, their loans are made to people who are building or buying homes. It's a simple and straightforward borrower-and-lender arrangement. The commercial banks, on the other hand, are the ones that can create money. And therein, as the saying goes, lies the tale.

Commercial banks today operate in much the same way as did the goldsmiths of a few hundred years ago—that is, banks know from experience that not all of their deposits are going to be drawn out at once. They need to keep only a fraction of their total deposits in reserve, but not all of them. Appropriately enough, then, we have what is known as a fractional reserve banking system. It works like this:

Suppose that a commercial bank has on hand checking account deposits that total $1,000. Such deposits in commercial banks sometimes are called the monetary base. Suppose further that the bank, by law, must keep in reserve a 15% fraction of its total deposits, or $150. That means, then, that the bank may regard remaining 85% of its deposits, or $850, as excess reserves and may loan that money out. And suppose that the bank does just that. The result is that a borrower is given a checking account with a balance of $850. Or, if the borrower already has a checking account at that bank, the balance is increased by $850 as a result of the loan. But that has not been done at the expense of the people who put the original $1,000 in the bank in the first place. They still have that much in their checking accounts, and they still can draw on it.

Now the main reason that people and businesses borrow is to buy something now for which they haven't saved enough money. Exactly how the spending is done, and how the money changes hands, also is part of the process of money creation. When a loan of this type is made, the bank generally credits the amount of the loan to the borrower's checking account. As soon as the bank has done that, its total deposits have risen to $1,850, an increase of $850. Now, just as the original $1,000 can serve as the basis for an 85% increase in the amount of money in the hands of spenders and buyers, so will this additional $850 serve as the basis for a similar increase in the total amount of money around if only 15% of it must be kept in reserve.

But wait a minute. Didn't we just say that the borrower borrowed the money in order to spend it for something? Well, if it's going to be spent on something, how can it serve as the basis for a further increase in the amount of money there is? The answer is that it doesn't matter which commercial bank the money is in. As soon as the borrower writes checks and spends the $850, thus reducing deposits at the first bank, it is going to go into other checking accounts—those of the sellers—in other banks, raising the deposits there. Deposits in the first bank may indeed go down by the full $850 that was created for the purposes of the loan to the borrower, but one or more other banks will see their deposits increase by that same $850. That is how that borrowed money, even though "spent," still can serve as the base for further increases in the supply of money.

Money creation is carried out by all commercial banks as a group.

The constant demand for lendable funds continues to create a demand for excess reserves until all excess reserves are gone and no more lending is possible. When does that happen? To determine that figure, divide the original $1,000 by .15, which represents the 15 cents out of every dollar of deposits that must be kept in reserve:

$1,000/.15 = $6,667.

Expansion can continue, therefore, until the original $1,000 has grown to $6,667, meaning that $5,667 has been added to what is called the money supply. In its broadest terms, the money supply includes

Coins.

Paper money.

Checking account deposits in commercial banks. (That is the part of the money supply in which the growth occurs.)

Savings accounts in commercial banks.

Deposits in savings and loan institutions and credit unions.

The need for balance

Earlier in this chapter, we listed some of the things for which new money is spent out in the economy. They include consumer products and machines, land, buildings, and manufacturing supplies. All of those things must be either built or in some way processed by people. And that means jobs. The ability of businesses to borrow money, at an affordable price (in other words, affordable interest rates), is necessary to have a healthy economy that provides jobs.

Well, you might be saying to yourself, if some of this money creation stuff is good, more must be better, and there can't possibly be too much. After all, more money means more jobs, and that takes care of your unemployment problem, right? Unfortunately, it doesn't work out quite that way, because the amount of new money being created and added to the economy must match, as closely as possible over the long term, the amount of new goods and services being produced and added to the economy. To increase the amount of money beyond the increase in the amount of goods and services available for sale will do nothing but inflate the money supply and raise prices. But as the output of the American economy grows and expands and as more goods and services are produced, the amount of money in the economy also must increase. How, then, is that done when all the excess reserves have been loaned out?

Recall that, in the example, the basis for the increase in the amount of money in the economy was the original $1,000 on deposit in the first commercial bank. If further lendable funds are needed, the thing to do is to come up with more deposits. And this can be done very easily.

Like any other modern nation, the United States has a central bank, the Federal Reserve Bank. The "Fed" is the federal government's bank, and it also performs certain services for commercial banks. One of the jobs of the Fed is to look after the country's supply of money. If the economy is to continue growing and providing jobs, the supply or amount of money in the economy must grow. It has to grow fast enough so that there is enough money to meet the borrowing needs of businesses and consumers, but not so fast that prices begin to rise. So how does the Fed do its job of supplying excess reserves to commercial banks?

Money creation

At the moment, the United States has quite a sizable national debt. An amount in the neighborhood of over 17 trillion dollars is a lot of money. The way the federal government borrowed that money was to sell bonds to people and businesses and to commercial banks and other financial intermediaries, who bought the interest-bearing bonds as a form of investment. One way to put more money into the hands of commercial banks so that they can continue the process of money creation is to buy back some of those bonds. The reason that works and the way it works is as follows:

When the Fed buys back government securities, the sellers are individuals and companies and commercial banks and all the other financial intermediaries. The sellers, of course, have to be paid, and here is where the additional excess reserves come from.

The Fed, as a bank, draws a check on itself and in doing so, literally creates the money to pay for the securities it is buying back. (This should not be confused with paying off the government's debt by buying back those securities with tax dollars.) The Fed's check is given to the seller of the securities. When the seller deposits that check in a commercial bank, the bank's deposits are increased by the amount of the check. To continue with the same numbers used in the example, the banks must keep only 15% of the amount of the check on deposit and may, therefore, loan out the other 85%. Thus, the amount of money in the economy can be increased once again.

80

Two things must be said about the process of money creation:

1. Creating money is a useful and necessary thing to do. If it is done improperly, however, a tremendous amount of harm can result. More about that in the next chapter.

2. Even though it is a good and useful process and even though it is done properly and carefully, it is not absolutely precise on a day-to-day basis. In our example, we were assuming that all of the money that the Fed paid out to purchase government securities back from investors went into checking accounts in commercial banks. We also assumed that the deposits that were to serve as the base for increasing the amount of money in circulation were used up and loaned out immediately and that all the money created was spent immediately. None of that is necessarily true. For example, some of the money from the buying back of securities by the government might wind up not in checking accounts but in savings accounts, which are part of the money supply, but not part of the money creation system. Some of the money from the sales of those securities might eventually wind up in the money creation system but not right away. There might be a time lag. Or possibly the increase or expansion might go along according to the example for the first two or three steps and then experience a lag.

We don't need the red ink

We've just explained how the Fed, by purchasing government securities, provides the deposits that the commercial banks use to increase the amount of money in circulation. That raises an interesting question: What would happen if the federal government not only balanced its budget, but ran a surplus for a few years, and paid off the national debt? What would happen if there were no more bonds or notes or bills or other forms of government securities out there for the Fed to buy back?

The answer is that there doesn't need to be all those government securities out there in the hands of investors so the Fed can buy them back to increase the money supply. The Fed simply could make a direct deposit into the commercial banking system with a check drawn on itself. That would provide the necessary basis for commercial banks to make loans and thereby create the additional money that is needed by consumers and businesses. We don't need the federal deficit for growth in the money supply.

The Fed

The Federal Reserve System, our country's central bank, is an independent monetary authority that was established in 1913 by the Federal Reserve Act. At the head of it is the seven-member Board of Governors. Each member of this board is appointed by the President of the United States, and confirmed by the Senate, to a term of fourteen years, a time period sufficient to give the board a long view and to minimize the influence on it of short-term political pressures. The Fed is divided into 12 districts: Atlanta, Boston, Chicago, Cleveland, Dallas, Kansas City, Minneapolis, New York, Philadelphia, Richmond, St. Louis, and San Francisco. Within those districts there are a total of 24 branches. Each of the twelve district banks has a nine-member board of directors: Three representing the member banks in that district and six representing the public. District banks get their income to operate from the interest they receive from government securities they hold. Each district bank is headed by a president, who is elected by the board of directors.

The Fed has several specific duties.

The most important thing that the Fed does is to control the money supply. That's what we've been talking about all along here, and we'll say more about it in the next chapter.

Another job the Fed does is to keep the country supplied with hand-to-hand money, both coins and paper currency. The paper money especially wears out from use, and the requirement for both kinds of money increases from time to time throughout the year. The Fed sees to it that commercial banks have enough coin and currency to meet the needs of the public.

The Fed also clears and collects the personal and payroll checks we all use, so that checks written by us, for example, are deposited in our creditor's accounts and deducted from our accounts.

The Fed holds the required reserves of commercial banks that are members of the Federal Reserve System. Commercial banks receive their charters, their permission to operate, either from the federal government or from a state government. The bank itself chooses whether it wants to be federally or state chartered. All federally chartered banks must belong to the Fed. State banks may if they wish. Of the approximately 12,000 commercial banks in this country, only about 4,700—about 3,700 federally chartered and about 1,000 state banks—are members. But the bulk of the country's demand deposits are in those commercial banks that are members of the Federal Reserve System.

The Fed is the U.S. government's bank. It is where the Treasury Department has its checking account.

Finally, the Fed supervises and regulates its member banks. It will conduct unannounced examinations of member banks' operations to see if they conform to accepted banking standards.

In summary, then, we've covered in this chapter that the mechanics of increasing the money supply are to be found in the commercial banking system. The cause and the cure of inflation, however, will be found in the area of politics. The solution, therefore, to the problem of inflation will be found not in the wallet, the paycheck, the corporate annual report, or the cash register. The solution to the problem of inflation will be found in the ballot box. We'll see why in the next chapter.

There is in this country at any one time a certain quantity of money. At the same time, there is a certain quantity of products for sale in the form of both goods and services. Now you might expect that for as long as the quantity of money in circulation in the economy, relative to the amount of products for sale in the economy, remains the same, *the general level of prices—the overall cost of living as measured in dollars per product* —would tend to remain the same. And it does. But as we all work from day-to-day and produce things on our jobs, we add products to the economy. If those products are to be bought and sold, then more dollars are going to have to be put into circulation.

Fortunately, as explained in the last chapter on banks, it is possible to create money. And as long as the quantity of money that is created and added to the economy matches the quantity of products that are being produced and added to the economy, it would seem reasonable that the general level—the overall average—of prices would tend to be stable. And under those conditions, it is. So what is happening when we see the prices of things in general rising rapidly? The answer is that for some reason, the balance between the number of the dollars in the economy and the quantity of products for sale in the economy has changed. There now are more dollars per product than there were before. The question is, why?

8 Inflation

(Until relatively recent times, our fears generally were focused on inflation being too high. And high inflation, along with the inevitable rising prices that accompany it, are a worry—and a serious one. That was our experience. For a half century, going back to the 1960s, an economic environment with real and serious inflationary potential was essentially the norm. And inflation was often the reality.

Over the past decade or so, however, concerns about inflation being too low also have materialized. Disinflation often indicates that an economy is weak and not growing at a healthy pace. So these days, regardless of which you choose to worry about, conditions can be found to accommodate your fears.

If it is true that you tend to fear the unknown more, then that would make disinflation more worrisome for you, because we have less experience with it, and less is known about it. Japan has been struggling with it for ten years, and they're still not out of the woods.

But too high a rate of inflation could be considered a much greater risk, given the historical prevalence of it and given any government's fundamental inclination to spend more than it has, borrow to cover the difference, and then repeat the cycle from one century into the next. We have more experience with inflation. And besides, right now no one is sure what to do about disinflation. So what's to say?

This chapter, then, will concentrate on inflation, *as opposed to* disinflation.*)*

When we talk about inflation in the only way that matters—that is, not as some abstract economic theory or some collection of numbers and percents, but as something that affects our daily lives—we are talking about a steady and sometimes rapid year-in, year-out increase in the general level of the prices—the number of dollars per product—of the things we buy: houses, cars, groceries, clothes, and so on.

The reason that all of those products are out there in the economy is that we, as consumers, have asked for them. Then we, as producers, have produced them. The reason that all that money is out there in the economy is so that we can use it as a tool to exchange what we produce for what we want to buy.

When commercial banks create money, that new money is loaned to both consumers and businesses for a great variety of purposes. That is how the new money gets out into the economy and is spent for the first time. The amount of money that banks can create, and then loan, depends on the amount of extra money that they have on deposit over and above what they need to handle day-to-day transactions for their customers, for check cashing and so on. The amount of excess reserves that a bank has can be increased by the Federal Reserve Bank, the nation's central bank, as explained in the last chapter when we talked about how the Fed purchases government securities. But the number of dollars that the Fed allows the banking system to create and add to the money supply—the growth in the money supply—must match, as closely as possible, the underlying, long-term growth in the amount of goods and services. When more dollars than that are added to the money supply, for whatever the reason, the general price level will rise.

The federal government—in fact, any government—has only one source of revenue: taxes. And taxes, of course, can come from only one source: The income of individual workers and savers. The tax might be in the form of a personal income tax or a sales tax, both of which are paid directly by the individual. But it also might be in the indirect form of a business tax, which (as discussed back in Chapter 4) must be covered in the selling price of the product, just the same as any other expense that a business incurs as it operates. And the selling price is, in the end, paid by the consumer. Also, what is paid out in taxes can't be paid in wages and can't be used to purchase tools.

Tax money, once collected, then is spent by the government on various

Things (buildings, automobiles, highways).

Services (public safety, public parks, national defense).

Programs that give money or goods directly to people (cash, food stamps, grants or subsidies, rent supplements).

Without arguing the rightness or the wrongness of any government expenditure or program (because it doesn't make any difference; the process is the same in all cases), the fact remains that no matter what the government spends money on, it first must take that money from the only source there is: Individuals who are working, producing, and earning a wage.

But what happens when the government's revenue falls short of its spending desires? In that case, the government, just the same as a business or a private individual, borrows. When the government borrows money, it sells securities—bonds or bills or notes—through the U.S. Treasury. Individuals, and institutions into which individuals have put their savings—banks, mutual funds, pension funds, insurance companies, all the financial intermediaries—purchase those securities as investments. The money to purchase those securities comes from checking account deposits in commercial banks in two ways:

1. Depositors, both individuals and financial intermediaries, write checks to the federal government.

2. The banks themselves, using some of their excess reserves, make loans to the government by purchasing its securities.

In either case, excess reserves that otherwise would serve as the basis for loans to businesses and consumers are loaned to and spent by the government. Also, what otherwise might have been put into a savings and loan institution to be available for mortgages has been loaned to the government to spend.

Nevertheless, so far, so good. No harm necessarily is done. What the government spends, whether it comes from taxes or from borrowed funds, is just that much less that the public has to spend. And up to a point, there is nothing wrong, as long as a couple of things don't happen:

As long as government spending doesn't require so much borrowing that there are not enough lendable funds left for businesses and consumers to meet their minimum needs. That sometimes is called "crowding out." It's not much of a worry these days, but it's something that can happen.

As long as the government doesn't try to replace the dollars it has borrowed by adding to the supply of money more newly created dollars than are needed to match the amount of goods and services being produced for sale in the economy. That sometimes is called "monetizing the national debt," and it is a completely different thing from repaying borrowed money with tax dollars. Again, not much of a worry right now, but it can happen.

The underlying principle

In the end, if money that the government has borrowed and spent is replaced in the economy through the purchase of government securities by the Fed, extra dollars are added to the ones that already are in circulation and that already match the goods and services that are available for sale. Existing purchasing power in the economy, which is the result of the effort and labor of working men and women, then is spread out over more individual dollars, meaning that each dollar has less purchasing power. The increase in the total number of dollars in circulation inflates the money supply and reduces the value, and therefore the purchasing power, of all dollars everywhere. That is what causes what we feel and refer to as inflation.

Inflation is caused by government spending when that spending is paid for not with taxes and not with borrowed money—both of which have real purchasing power—but with new dollars that are not matched by newly produced goods and services.

This, then, explains why it is possible for people to earn more but still find it difficult to make ends meet. It explains why people can say that "the money supply is growing too fast," but any extra dollars that you might find in your pocket or purse aren't doing you much real good.

It explains what the expression "keeping the government printing presses running overtime" means. And it explains what the expression "too many dollars chasing too few goods" means.

The actual mathematics of inflation is straightforward. Consider that the price of anything is a fraction, with number of dollars in the numerator and quantity of product in the denominator. It is written as

$$\text{Price of anything} = \frac{\text{dollars}}{\text{product}}$$

If, for example, the price is one dollar for two ballpoint pens, then

$$\text{Price of a ballpoint pen} = \frac{\text{one dollar}}{\text{two pens}} = \$.50 \text{ per pen}$$

And what is true for a single item serves as a good way to explain what happens with all items in a country's economy. So,

$$\text{Price of everything} = \frac{\text{all dollars}}{\text{all products}}$$

Now what happens to the value of a fraction when you multiply both the numerator and the denominator by the same number? For instance,

$$\frac{1}{4} = .25$$

$$\frac{1 \times 2}{4 \times 2} = \frac{2}{8} = \frac{1}{4} = .25$$

The result is that nothing happens. The value of the fraction remains unchanged.

What happens, however, if you multiply the numerator by a larger number than you use to multiply the denominator?

$$\frac{1}{4} \times \frac{4}{2} = \frac{4}{8} = \frac{1}{2} = .50$$

The value of the fraction increases.

That brings us to the point of this brief exercise in fractions:

When you increase the number of dollars in a national economy faster than you increase the quantity of goods and services for sale in that economy, the average level of prices will rise. Another way of saying it is that the cost of living goes up, or *you have inflation.*

In his 1992 book, Money Mischief,[3] Nobel economist Milton Friedman showed graphically the relationship between money and prices in the United States, the United Kingdom, Germany, Japan, and Brazil. That data is presented here in Figures 1 through 5.

---

[3] Excerpt and graphs from MONEY MISCHIEF: EPISODES IN MONETARY HISTORY copyright 1992 by Milton Friedman reprinted by permission of Harcourt, Brace, and Jovanovich, Inc.

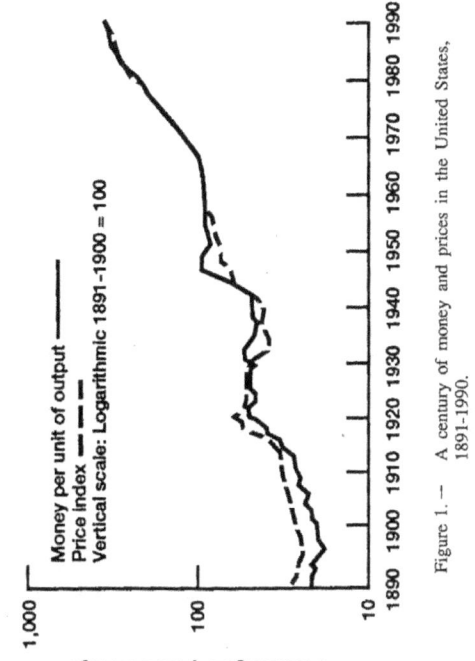

Figure 1. —   A century of money and prices in the United States, 1891-1990.

91

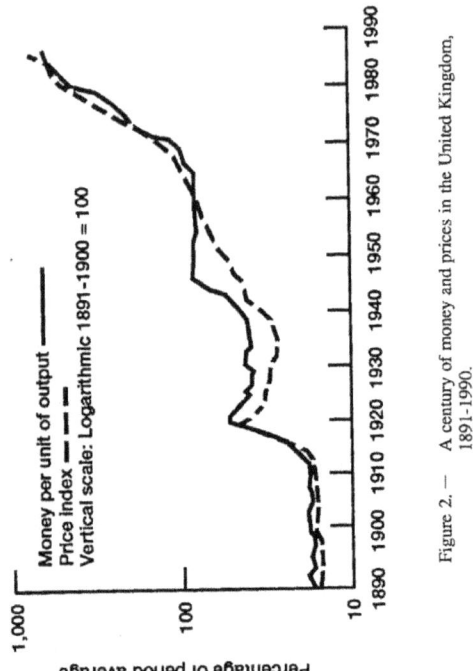

Figure 2. — A century of money and prices in the United Kingdom, 1891-1990.

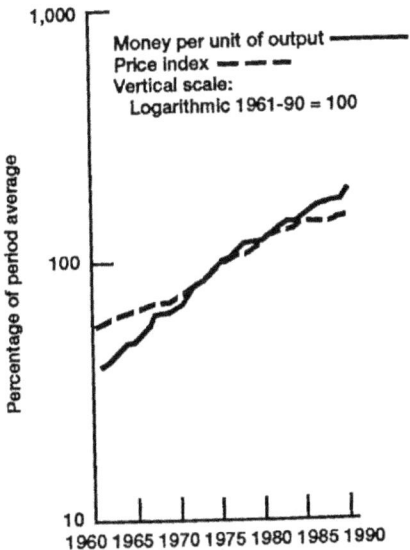

Figure 3. — Three decades of money and prices in Germany, 1961-1990.

93

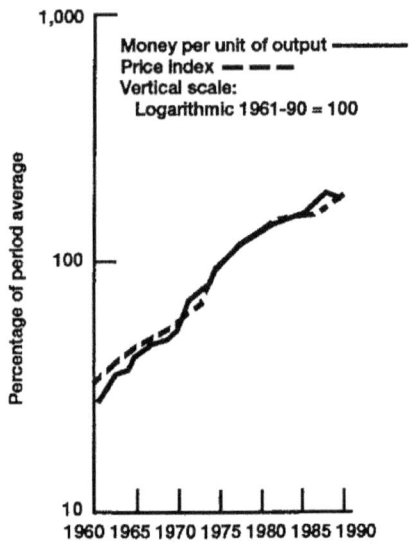

Figure 4. —   Three decades of money and prices in Japan, 1961-
1990.

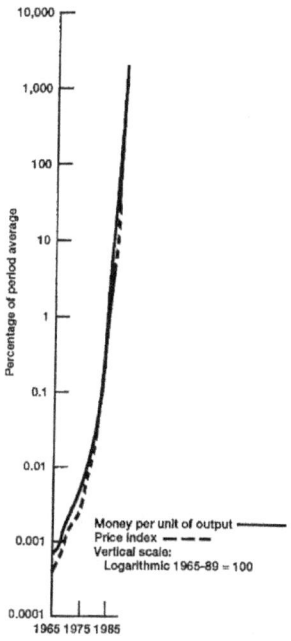

Figure 5. — A quarter century of inflation in Brazil, 1965-1989.

As Prof. Friedman explains, "Inflation occurs when the quantity of money rises appreciably more rapidly than output [which he already has defined as the quantity of goods and services available for purchase], and the more rapid the rise in the quantity of money per unit of output, the

95

greater the rate of inflation. There is probably no other proposition in economics that is as well-established as this one."

Well, if *that* is what causes inflation, what about all of the other reasons that are offered so frequently, such as:

Price increases by manufacturers and producers
Outsize wage settlements
Greedy oil sheikhs
Greedy middlemen.
Spendthrift consumers
Lousy weather
Declining productivity

The first four items will have an obvious effect on prices of individual products.

A manufacturer may think a certain product is worth more than its current price.

A new labor contract may have increased wage costs, which then are passed through to the consumer.

Higher oil prices may increase production costs either because energy costs have risen generally or because raw material costs have risen due to higher prices for the petroleum feedstocks that are used to manufacture a product.

Middlemen may charge more for the services they perform.

Now, if the increase in the price of some single item, due to any of the above reasons, is small or modest, one of two things, or some of each, will happen:

1. **Sales of that item will drop off.** If consumers can afford to spend only so many dollars, in total, on a particular product, and if suddenly that product requires more dollars to purchase, then the number of those individual products bought will decline. This is an

example of what is called elastic demand. The demand for the product changes with the price.

2. **Sales of other items will drop off.** If consumers continue to buy the same total quantity of a particular product, even though the individual price of that product has gone up, dollars that were being spent on other things now will be spent on that product, and sales of other items will go down. This is an example of what is called inelastic demand: The demand for the product does not change with the price.

But either way, if there aren't extra dollars added to the economy, the overall average level of prices will remain the same.

Suppose, however, that there is an increase in the price of some key item in the economy and that the increase is a whopper! Take, for example, the very sharp increase in the price of oil in 1973. That increase was so sudden and so severe that to do nothing to the money supply would have meant disaster. Because so many more dollars now had to be spent on petroleum, both as a source of energy and as a manufacturing raw material, not nearly enough dollars would have been left for the buying and selling of all the other items in the economy. We would not have had enough of that important tool—money—so that both consumers and businesses could meet their needs and keep economic activity, and employment, at, or even near, normal levels.

So what happened? The Fed had to add to the money supply extra dollars beyond those that already matched the goods and services that were being produced. That way, the huge quantities of dollars that were necessary for transactions involving petroleum did not have to come at the expense of transactions involving all other goods and services in the economy.

What was the result? Those extra dollars then worked their way into the economy and gave an upward push to the overall average of the prices of all the things we buy.

But was that inflation? It certainly was an example of rising prices, but was it really inflation? When we talk about inflation, we're talking about the result of steady year-in, year-out increases in the money supply to finance government spending that is not being paid for with taxes or with borrowed money. The oil price increase, even though it was severe and even though it caused a general price rise, was a single event that was separate from government fiscal policies.

As for the last three items in the list, consumers can indulge in spendthrift habits, and in the process tend to bid up prices, but only for so long. Eventually, they're tapped out, the spree comes to an end, demand falls back, and prices will tend to return to where they were. It's a temporary thing.

Essentially the same thing is true if bad weather reduces the supply and increases the price of some agricultural product. When another harvest comes to market and the supply increases, prices drop. All of us have seen that happen every so often when there's too little rain or too much rain or it's too hot or too cold or whatever. It's a temporary thing.

What about declining productivity? Declining productivity means that because our tools are becoming either worn out or obsolete or both, we are able to produce fewer goods and services by our efforts and we wind up living less well than we did before. The effect of inflation is that because our money wage won't go as far this year as it did last year, our efforts, as represented by our money, are able to obtain fewer goods and services for us. And we live less well.

But there is one difference that enables us to tell the effects of declining productivity from the effects of inflation, and that is that inflation, as the term implies, involves inflating the money supply with more new dollars than are needed to match the output of new goods and services. The effect of inflation generally is more rapid and more severe. As indicated back in Chapter 3, it takes a while for insufficient saving for tools to make itself felt. That's what's so dangerous about it. Its effects sneak up on you, and all of a sudden you wake up and realize that you are at a distinct competitive disadvantage in your markets. Productivity will not decline by 13.5% in one year, the way prices jumped in the United States in the year 1979.

Can any of the seven factors listed have any effect on prices at all? Yes, but not with the kind of steady, long term, and sometimes rapid upward push on all prices that a constant and steady excessive increase in the supply of money can have.

Because none of the "causes" listed above really produces inflation, it should come as no surprise that such things as wage and price controls, gasoline allocations, income tax surcharges (to take money out of the hands of spendthrift consumers), and blue ribbon federal commissions studying productivity can't cure inflation. That's why it isn't enough to know that prices are rising. You need to know *why* they are rising.

No matter what, it's extra dollars that cause the general level of prices to rise under any circumstances. But it is the sustained and continuous addition to the money supply of excess dollars, which are used to finance part of the government's spending, that causes the sustained and continuous rise in the prices of the things we buy, that causes inflation. The solution, therefore, to the problem of inflation is to not add those dollars to the money supply and either reduce government spending to a level that we generally are willing to pay cash for, or raise taxes so that we generally pay cash for whatever the government spends.

Some flexibility in the federal budget under certain circumstances is, of course, desirable and necessary, but there's no substitute, over the long haul, for living within our means, because there is no way to avoid paying, eventually, one way or another, for what we buy.

Learning about money creation, commercial banks, and the Federal Reserve System will provide answers to the questions *What* is inflation? and *How* is it caused? That's the economics part of our lives that involves us as producers and wage earners, and as spenders and savers of our money. It is to the political part of our lives, however, the part that involves us as voters, that we must look for an answer to the question, *Why* do we have inflation? The answer is that we, the voters, allow our government to create it. To say anything else is to deny that America is a democracy and that Americans are free men and women who control their own lives and who are in ultimate charge of the size, the scope, and the spending practices of their own government.

Epilogue

In the five-year period from 2009 through 2013, the Federal Reserve, in an attempt to stimulate economic activity, added approximately $3.5 trillion to the commercial banking system by buying back government securities. And that is a *lot* of dollars. What that should have meant, phrasing things in terms of the price fraction--dollars in the economy per products for sale in the economy--is that the numerator was increasing dramatically, but the denominator was not. Suddenly, there were more dollars being made available to chase fewer goods and services. So why was there not great inflation?

One explanation that has been offered is that when the economy is not strong, and consumer demand is not strong either, there will be little, if any, upward pressure on prices.

Another reason put forth involves the "money multiplier," which was covered in Chapter 7 in the section on money creation. Banks did not lend out the excess reserves that the Fed had added to the commercial banking system. They, the banks, held their excess reserves, which did not then become the basis for additions to the money supply through loans. So there actually were *not* so many more dollars put out into the economy to chase fewer goods and services.

Precise answers are hard to come by, because there is not much precedent for this kind of situation. So at the moment, all that can be said is the obvious: Banks are holding their excess reserves instead of loaning them out.

None of this, however, invalidates the fundamental proposition that when dollars *are* being added to the economy at a faster rate than goods and services are being produced for sale, prices will rise because the money supply becomes inflated.

In the previous chapter, when we covered inflation, we talked about one of the two most dreaded and harmful things that can happen to wage earners: The destruction of the purchasing power of the income they have earned by their efforts. Now we're going to cover the other: No wage at all. This chapter, in all probability, is not going to do what you might be expecting it to do—that is, it is not going to offer a cure for unemployment. That you already know. The one and only cure for anyone's unemployment is a job doing real work that someone else will pay real money to have done. This chapter will, however, be interesting.

9 Unemployment

In the third chapter, the one on capital, we were talking about what this country was like in the 1800s. At that time, nearly all of us were farmers living on our own land and using our own tools to provide ourselves directly with most of what we needed to live. Suppose that at that time, a family were to wake up one morning and find that all of their tools were gone--the mule, the plow, all of the hand tools. Everything. If that had happened, their ability to provide themselves with the food, clothing, and shelter that they needed would have been reduced severely. They might have been able to scratch around and do a few things with their hands, but not much.

Today, a person without a job is in very much the same situation. Without an employer, he hasn't any tools to use to do useful, productive work so he can convert his effort into a money wage to provide for himself and his family. Today, a person without a job, like the farmer in the 1800s without a plow, has labor to offer, but no opportunity to connect it up with tools to produce anything useful. Back in the 1800s, such a situation was called "hard times." Today, it's called "unemployment."

The numbers

The development of the figure that is called the unemployment rate is the job of the Bureau of Labor Statistics of the U.S. Department of Labor. The whole process starts with interviews that are conducted each month with a sample of the population of the United States. That sample consists of 60,000 households, which, taken together, provide a representative picture of what's going on in the country as a whole. The households in the sample are rotated, changed, and finally dropped altogether and replaced on a regular basis by other households.

The data is gathered by interviewers who actually visit each household in the sample, ask the same questions in the same way, and record the answers that are given on a standard form. That information then is processed by computer to finally produce the monthly figure that is published as the country's unemployment rate. The data is gathered in such a way that every person over the age of 16 years, who is not in a prison, a mental hospital, or some other institution, can be classified and reported as employed, unemployed, or not in the labor force.

At a first glance, the meaning of the terms "employed" and "unemployed" and the difference between the two of them would seem obvious to anyone. If it ever has happened to you, you probably didn't have any trouble at all telling the difference between having a job one day and not having one the next. Unemployment occurred when you could not find a market, a buyer, for your labor. (That didn't necessarily mean that there was no market. What it did mean was that right then and there at that time, you, a seller of labor, and an employer, a buyer, couldn't find each other.)

Now, when we talk about an individual wage earner, who may have a family to support and all of the usual financial obligations, everything is pretty clear and straightforward. But when the labor force is taken as a whole, and we start looking at numbers and statistics and all the rest, a funny thing happens. All of a sudden you start to see a lot of other people in the "unemployed" category that you wouldn't expect to find there.

All in the same boat?

The labor force in the United States today has over 155 million people in it. When the unemployment rate is, for example, 6.3%, that generally is interpreted to mean that about 9.8 million people in this country, who need work, have been turned out of their jobs through no fault of their own. But is that really the case? Let's take a look at a few examples.

Ed was a machinist in a medium-size tool and die company. He's 30 years old, married, and is the father of three children, ages 4, 6, and 9 years. He had served his apprenticeship in the die room of a local plant that was part of a large national manufacturing company. He made the job change because, all things considered, it was a much better opportunity for him. Ed's wife and their three children were happy about the move because it meant that Ed now would be working first shift, and they all could be together more of the time. And there also was a better chance for advancement and more money.

Ed's new boss was genuinely sorry to have to lay him off. Ed was a smart, skilled, steady employee. But business had fallen off so much that there was hardly enough work to keep some of the 20-year employees going, and Ed had been there less than two years. Ed, of course, has all of the usual bills to pay and other financial obligations to take care of: House and car payments, utilities, food, clothing, insurance, and on and on. He's worrying now about finding some sort of worthwhile job as quickly as possible. Yes, Ed is drawing unemployment compensation, but that isn't the same as a steady paycheck.

Ed's boss wished him well when he left, but on the other hand, the company is afraid they might not see Ed again when things pick up if he finds a good job somewhere else. All around, it's a bad situation, for Ed and for the company.

Ed is unemployed. He's in the monthly Labor Department statistics as part of the unemployment rate.

Then there's Grace. She and her husband Bill have been married for 30 years now and have paid for their home. Bill has had a good job for over 32 years, and the two of them are doing quite well. The older of their two daughters has just married and moved out for good. The younger daughter is away at school. The house is pretty empty now.

Grace has plenty of time on her hands, and she could stand to have something to do. And the more she thinks back about it, the more she remembers how much she liked the job she had before she married Bill and the family came along. She doesn't regret her decision to become a full-time homemaker. She just remembers liking her job, and she's convinced that she could find something interesting and challenging to do with very little trouble. Her business skills may be a little rusty, but they've not been forgotten by any means. Some brushing up is all that's needed. That settles it! She's going to answer some of the want ads in today's paper.

Grace obviously doesn't need the money. She's a little lonesome right now. Actually, she's bored to death. But she shows up in the monthly statistics just the same. All of a sudden, Grace is one of the unemployed.

But look at Mildred. She's married, too. Her husband, Jack, had a good job, and when little Jackie came along, they liked him to much that they wanted two or three more. That's pretty unlikely now. Jack can't work anymore since the automobile accident. Yes, there's the disability money, but it isn't enough really, and so Mildred went out and got a job three years ago.

That is she had a job until the little company where she was working closed its doors for good. Sure, there was severance pay. In fact, the owners were pretty generous. But that won't last forever.

Mildred, too, has just joined the ranks of the unemployed.

Now let's look at Rick. He's 20 years old and still lives at home. He's been working since he graduated from high school two years ago, but the job he has is a dead-ender. And his boss is a creep. Besides, he's managed to save a good bit of what he's earned, he owns his car, and he doesn't need that much money anyhow. So what's the big deal? Rick decides to quit his job, and while he's relaxing, he can start applying to a few places where some of his friends work. They all seem to like what they're doing. Maybe he will, too. Maybe he can land an apprenticeship somewhere.

His old company puts him down in its records as "Voluntary quit. Would rehire." The federal government puts him down in its records as unemployed.

Finally, we come to Frankie. Good old Frankie. He's his own man. He's independent, he likes his freedom, and nobody is going to tell him what to do—not even to stay in school past his sixteenth birthday. His sixteenth birthday was yesterday, and all of a sudden, when he's not in school, Frankie isn't playing hooky or goofing off any more. He's unemployed.

Naturally, Frankie hasn't any skills, so he's not particularly desirable as a potential employee, and it very probably will be some time before he finds work. But Frankie has qualified, according to the standards the government has set, to be considered as unemployed, because he is over sixteen, says he's looking for full-time work, but can't find a job. (He still works a few hours a week for a couple of afternoons and on Saturday, the way he did when he was in school. But he's not working enough to keep him from being classified as unemployed.)

What we've been talking about so far here are five people in very different sets of circumstances. Based on what we know, two of them, Ed and Mildred, need money badly. But the other three, Grace, Rick, and Frankie, are far from desperate.

Ed and Mildred have other people who depend on them for support, people who can't take care of themselves. Grace, Rick, and Frankie haven't any financial obligations at all.

Ed and Mildred are up against it because of events over which they had no control. Grace, Rick, and Frankie decided to do what they did voluntarily. There is one thing, however, that they all have in common:

As far as the federal government and its statistics are concerned, they're all just "unemployed"—period. By the time the five of them are counted and processed and shuffled into the statistics, you can't tell one from another.

There are, of course, a lot of other examples of people in many other types of situations who are included in government statistics under the heading "unemployed." But by now, you get the idea: The statistics are not what they seem to be at first glance. (One thing should be pointed out: Not everyone who is considered to be "unemployed" is eligible for unemployment compensation.) So what does it all mean? Simply this:

The unemployment rate that is published each month is *not* a measure of hardship only. It is a figure that shows how many people who say that they are looking for a job can't find one, whether or not they are hard up, loaded with dependents, desperate for money, or glad of the opportunity to sit back and relax for a little while. It also doesn't matter whether they've been out of work for two weeks or five months.

So, how does all of this affect the actual published figures? Let's pick a month and see. Take May 2014, for example. That month, the total labor force amounted to 155,613,000 and the number of people employed as 145,814,000. That meant that there were 9,799,000 people classified by the Labor Department as unemployed. The unemployment rate was 6.3%

But who, exactly, were those people?

A very mixed bag

Of the total 9,799,000 people listed as unemployed, 1,062,000 were "new entrants"—most of them young, just out of school, and looking for their first job. (Or maybe high school dropouts like our friend Frankie.)

Another 2,857,000 were people going back into the job market after being out for some length of time. (Perhaps like Grace.)

And another 875,000 left their jobs voluntarily for one reason or another. (Maybe like Rick.)

So what do we have so far?

Out of a total of 9,799,000 individuals listed by the Labor Department as unemployed, nearly half that amount, 4,794,000, have *not* been thrown out of work. This doesn't mean that they shouldn't be working or have no business looking for a job. It just means that they weren't kicked out of a job against their will. Why, then are all those people just lumped together?

The unemployment rate that is compiled and published each month by the Department of Labor and that you find in the news is just like any other statistic: What it tells you depends entirely on what sort of information you include when you are gathering the data and adding things up. Consider another familiar statistic, a baseball player's batting average. That figure is calculated by dividing the number of hits that a player gets—whether they are singles, doubles, triples, or home runs—by the number of times he is at bat—except for those times at the plate when he draws a walk. But . . .

Why shouldn't a home run be worth more to a player's average than a single? Why not measure a player's performance by his on-base percentage, which is the total number of hits and walks divided by the number of times at bat? No matter how he gets to first base, a player can score once he's there. There probably are dozens—maybe hundreds—of other similar questions that could be asked about baseball statistics in general, but the answer would be the same every time: That's the way someone decided to do it.

And exactly the same thing is true of the unemployment figures: What they tell you depends on what information is included in them. At some time in the past, someone in the Bureau of Labor Statistics of the U.S. Department of Labor sat down and said, "Yes, we'll include these people over here in these particular circumstances," and "No, we won't include those people over there in those particular circumstances."

To return to the figures of May 2014, if we subtract the 4,794,000 people who were *not* thrown out of work, from the total of 9,799,000 people who listed as unemployed, we have only 5,005,000 people who were laid off or otherwise put out of their jobs involuntarily.

That means that the unemployment rate for people who were thrown out of work is 3.2%, or only a bit more than half the published figure of 6.3%. Are those who are part of that 3.2% any better off because there are fewer of them than we thought? No, of course not. What it does mean is that involuntary unemployment is not as great as it seems to be.

But the published unemployment figures affect you even if you *are* working. Unemployment frequently is turned into an extremely emotional political issue that results, very often, in federal "job creation" and other programs that have a very appealing sound to them. How well have those programs done? By and large, the news media tell the same story over and over again: It's difficult to find anyone, including the participants in the programs, who would call them genuinely successful. They'd much rather be getting a real wage for doing real work. Such programs do, however, consume tremendous sums of tax dollars.

When all is said and done, the most useful thing that any government can do to keep unemployment to a minimum is to maintain an atmosphere in which producers of goods and services can thrive and thus create real, wage-paying jobs. That, in turn, will happen when prosperous consumers with a minimum tax burden are creating a demand for those same goods and services.

10 A Look Back—and a Look Ahead

We've covered the basics of what we have here in America and how we've accomplished it and why it's good. So where does that put us right now? What should we be thinking about? Where should we be looking? What should we be seeing?

The United States of America, our country, is going through a difficult time right now. There are indications that things could get worse before they get better. In fact, there are indications that they could get worse permanently. And it's not just a matter of trying to struggle out of The Great Recession. It's a matter of the fundamental direction in which our country is headed—the size of our government, the huge expense of our government, the extent of our government's involvement in our daily lives. Our country's Founders never could have imagined what we have today. We have people who are being paid a living wage by our government to decide, for parents, whether their children should be allowed to drink chocolate milk in school. That is not good. That is, in fact, embarrassing. That kind of thing is worthy of the old Soviet Union. And we used to make fun of those guys.

We're not in irreversible trouble yet, and we still have a little time. But we do stand at a crossroads, and we, as a country, need to make some decisions about some very important issues. But to do that, we need to take an interest in things, in what we have and how it all came about. We need to consider and appreciate what America has achieved in a mere two and a half centuries of political and economic freedom, for us and for the world as well.

Now, if you are expecting, at this point, to be given a list of specific things to concern yourself with and worry about, and then a crib sheet to tell you how to vote on each one of them, forget that. It's not going to be that easy, because in a democracy, it never is. Freedom in a democracy means taking responsibility for doing what needs to be done so that things come out right.

You know by this time what the main principles of operation of our country are:

111

1. America's wealth and prosperity come only from the productive output of America's working men and women, no matter what they do. What we have—all that we have —is what we ourselves produce.

2. And from that, it follows very obviously that no matter what our government wants to spend on anyone or anything, it first must take from the only source of wealth there is: The money of those who have worked, produced, and thereby earned a wage that can be taxed. The government itself, the bureaucracy, is a source of nothing.

3. The only way our society, or any other society, progresses and advances to the benefit of its working men and women is by saving a portion of what we have produced today but can do without today. Those savings are used to acquire tools, capital equipment, the devices that allow us to multiply our human effort so we can raise our standard of living and improve our quality of life. Call it capital accumulation or retained earnings or not eating the seed corn or whatever you want to call it. It amounts to the same thing.

4. Finally, there is our Constitution, which gives us our system of government and guarantees us not only political liberty but economic freedom as well. And that is something that distinguishes us not only from the rest of the world today, but from any other country in history. There never before has been, and there is nothing today, anything like us, anything like the United States of America.

And very conspicuous by their absence from that short list of fundamental principles are government activities that go far beyond protecting the rights of its citizens and that are financed by the kind of massive deficit spending that has become government policy and an accepted way of life. Accepted by whom? By us, of course, because we are in ultimate charge.

Americans have lost sight of the fact that we, "We the People of the United States...," live in a democracy, and because of that, our government is one that "...[derives its] just powers from the consent of the governed...." From us. (Those are, by now, two familiar quotations, but they bear repeating here, because they definitely apply.) We don't have to put up with a government that is pushing us ever closer to European socialism and adding to a federal debt that will disgrace us in the eyes of our children and humiliate us in the eyes of history.

In the 1980's, America's total accumulated national debt passed the $1-trillion mark. That was fairly big news at the time. A mere quarter of a century later, however, we began to overspend by more than that amount in a single year. In 2009, the government ran a deficit of nearly $1.5 trillion. The deficits for the next three years also were over $1 trillion. Then things tapered off a bit, and for a while, it took us two years to overspend by a trillion dollars. But there is no need to worry that our government has instituted a policy of rigid austerity measures, because current projections call for the annual deficit to begin climbing back again to the trillion-dollar level over the next few years. In other words, we once again will be adding to our total national debt in one year what it had taken two centuries for us to accumulate. That is what we are leaving our children, and they will not be able to get out from under it by saying that they didn't run up the bills. They'll be stuck with our debt, and nothing they can do about it. To paraphrase a well-known passage from the Bible, Be not deceived. Our debt will not go away. For whatsoever this generation borrows and spends, our children must repay—with interest.

Recall what Thomas Jefferson said at the end of Chapter 2, about "...a wise and frugal government, which shall restrain men from injuring one another, which shall leave them otherwise free to regulate their own pursuits of industry and improvement, and shall not take from the mouth of labor the bread it has earned." Recall also what was said about our government being formed to protect our unalienable rights; to protect our property so we can feel secure in our homes; to enforce contracts freely made between individuals; and to otherwise allow us to live our lives in peace and freedom. That is not what we have today.

The real reason for lobbying

Talk of government spending frequently leads to the subject of lobbying, and periodically, there is some sort of flap in the news, mainly complaining about how much of it there is. But lobbying really is the most normal, natural, and in some unfortunate cases, the most necessary thing in the world, and it tells us something very important: Lobbying exists to the extent that it does in this country—and there is a lot of it — because the government is so deeply involved in so many things. If there were not as many opportunities as there are for the government to impose regulations, give waivers, let contracts, and grant favors, there would be a lot less lobbying, because there would be a lot less occasion for it.

A zero-sum game

The idea that there is a very great difference between the way economic growth occurs and the way government growth occurs is important to recognize.

Economic growth occurs because new wealth has been created. There is stuff around now that didn't exist before. And this stuff is there because working men and women have done something: They have taken what they have found in nature, and they have changed it somehow. The result is that we have all of the goods and services that we see all around us. Not everyone has the same amount, to be sure, but without question there is more available for everyone. That is possible because *economic potential is not fixed.* It can grow. New goods and services can be created. That is the story of human progress throughout history, the story of the improvement in the human condition. The economic pie gets bigger. We can make it so. And we do.

We produce more partly by working harder and more diligently, but mainly by working smarter and more cleverly with more and better use of more and better tools. Capital. That means that everyone can have more without anyone being required to give something up and do with less. We bake the bigger pie. Nowhere is that better and more clearly exemplified than here in our own country by the existence of this huge and prosperous middle class that pretty much *is* working, producing America.

Growth in government, however, is an entirely different and essentially opposite matter, because the amount of political power *is* fixed. In America or anywhere else. Again referring to the Declaration of Independence, we "...are endowed by [our] Creator with certain unalienable Rights.... That to secure these rights, Governments are instituted among Men, *deriving their just powers from the consent of the governed...*." (Italics added.) That means that we each have our own share of personal and individual political power, and that's all there is in total, and if anyone wants more, it *must* come from the rest of us, because it doesn't exist anywhere else, and we can't produce more ourselves.

So we form these governments, and we voluntarily give up to them a certain amount of our own inherent and personal power. For example, we don't mind giving up a little bit of our freedom for the sake of order and personal safety. Who would want to live in a town full of four-way intersections with no stop signs or traffic lights? Staying alive would be challenging, to say the least. So we voluntarily empower our government to devise ways to control the flow of traffic so that we all stand a decent chance of getting where we're going in one piece. And when we look around us and see that kind of thing, we understand the reasonableness and the necessity of what we see, and we're OK with it.

But today, when we look toward our nation's capital and see what our federal government has become, it's quite a different matter. Such phrases as "bloated bureaucracy" and "out-of-control spending" and "regulatory nightmare" come to mind. And if we don't shake our heads in despair, we find ourselves rolling our eyes in hopelessness as we see and think about the sheer size, the magnitude, and the almost incredible reach and penetration of federal involvement in our own daily lives.

How did it happen? Upon what meat has this our government fed that it has grown so great? It has happened because Americans have lost sight of the fact that all of the political power that exists in America really is theirs, *and* it's a fixed amount. The power they see in Washington has come from them and from nowhere else. It has been a gradual process that has been going on in earnest now for decades. The government has become greater, and we--each of us and all of us--have become smaller. Economic growth creates and contributes. Government growth consumes—both wealth and individual freedom.

Political power really is a zero-sum game.

Other considerations

America's importance in the world today must not be underestimated, and indeed cannot be overstated. The world is a far better place for everyone—especially us Americans—because we have thus far kept pretty true to the shining ideals and the moral high-mindedness that guided the Founders at the time of this country's birth. And it is not stretching things at all to say that "We the people…," the working, producing, and earning men and women of America, are the best and only hope for America, and that America is, realistically, the best and only hope for the world.

And that idea of us being our only hope is not a redundancy. The people we elect may represent us and conduct some of our business for us, but we are the ones who actually do things: Come up with new ideas, push those ideas and nurse them along until they become some new product or service that didn't exist before, and make things better than they were. Just think about the contributions of Eli Whitney, Cyrus McCormick, Thomas Edison, Henry Ford, and Steve Jobs.

This chapter began with a few questions about where we should be looking and what we should be seeing. One direction in which we should be looking if we want to take any sort of "long view" ahead for America is eastward across the Atlantic Ocean. What we will see will be not only most enlightening but quite usefully frightening as well, provided that we really understand what we are looking at, and that is this: The fiscal crisis in Europe is to America what the Ghost of Christmas Yet To Come was to Ebenezer Scrooge: The very nearly guaranteed future for us if we keep on going the way we're going right now. European socialism finally has got to where it has been heading all along, and that is the path along which we here in America now tread. And whether they're in the news or out of the news, Europe's fiscal problems are still there, because they surely haven't been solved.

(Actually, European socialism in general has not been much in the news in 2015 for two reasons. One is the immigration crisis, which is no small matter. The second reason—and by far the more important one for the purposes of this discussion—is that Greece has been stealing the

116

spotlight from the rest of Europe, because its problems are so conspicuously severe and essentially unprecedented.

Greece has got to where the rest of Europe is heading and where some countries there have nearly arrived. Greece cannot borrow money on its own, because no one believes that it ever will be able to repay the loan itself, much less the interest. Greece could offer bonds to investors at 1,000% interest and still would find no buyers, because everyone understands that 1,000% of nothing is nothing. So, the money that Greece is receiving is more like a handout than a loan. No one expects Greece to repay anything on schedule—or perhaps ever.)

Americans need to focus on where everything they have around them that is good and plentiful has come from. We need to be aware of how we have achieved the prosperity that brings with it our security and comfort and peace of mind. And what will—or will not—keep it for us. The American economy, its productive capacity, is finite. It has limits. It can break from misuse and overload.

And to those who think that nothing bad probably ever will happen in Europe and surely never will happen in America, something bad already has happened to a former world power that is highly visible and quite predictive of what could happen here in America.

The Soviet Union crumbled into non-existence a short quarter century ago, because its economy became so overspent and so overloaded that it finally just collapsed. America is moving in that direction right now. With the Soviets, it was military spending. For America, as it has been with Europe, it is an ever expanding and ever more costly government with programs that intrude ever more deeply into the lives of all Americans and simply don't produce the beneficial results that are promised to us. Because they simply can't.

The world is largely free today because in the middle of the last century, America was able to rise to the challenge of being the Arsenal of Democracy. Today, Americans must rise to another challenge if we are to avoid ever greater usurpation of our fundamental freedoms by an ever enlarging and more costly government bureaucracy: We must preserve our personal freedoms and our personal and national economic capacity to remain strong by becoming the Arsenal of Capitalism.

How important is all of this? To Americans? To the rest of the world? Very nearly beyond telling. From its birth, America always has been the best hope of mankind. That is not surprising, given the system of government that was created by the Founders. Their uprightness of character and probity virtually guaranteed it. But today it is the final and only hope. Again, consider Europe to observe not merely the failure of socialism and its unrestrained government spending, but the horror of it as well as all of the accumulated bills come due. And no way to pay them now anymore without truly great discomfort. Sooner or later, Europeans are going to have to sustain a very painful punch in the pocketbook, because they must pay at some point for what they already have bought on credit and consumed. Their debt cannot be repudiated by just writing it off the books. Neither can ours.

Why should we care? Look at Europe today, see America tomorrow. How can we miss it, as we are doing? How can we not see it, when it's right there in front of our eyes? The answer is easy: We simply have not been taking an interest in national issues that are vitally important not just to us as a country, where it's all sort of spread out and not tightly focused, but to us personally and to our families.

Two and a half centuries ago, the Founders of our country put their lives, their fortunes, and their sacred honor on the line. Then they put their trust in God. The colonists endured hardships during the nearly decade-long Revolutionary War that we can't begin to imagine today. Many thousands gave their lives. Since then, millions have fought and hundreds of thousands have died to preserve—for us—the life we have today. It does not overstate things at all to say that we are at some real risk of losing it all now. Losing what, precisely? We will have lost not merely our own prosperity and our capacity to do good for others. We will have lost our own honor, our own self-respect, and any claim we might have had on the respect of our children. They would never look at us as we now look at the Founders or, more recently, at what has come to be known as the Greatest Generation, whose children, whose heirs, whose beneficiaries we are.

118

We have a challenge today, but even more, even better, we have our own opportunity to do good, to do the right thing, to be American heroes in our own time, to truly follow in the footsteps of the Founders. In fact, we have a duty: To preserve, not just for ourselves but for all of mankind, present and future, the economic system that has allowed America to do more palpable good for more people than any other human endeavor in the history of the world. But whereas it is true that America is unique, we are not alone. No matter what happens to us, the rest of the world will be right there with us, prospering or suffering.

But there will be something new and different, for the world in general and for Americans in particular, if the United States as a country should lose its economic strength and independence, and lose with it our historic ability to stand tall and stand alone: America will know for the first time what it is like in some hour of need to look to itself and find the cupboard bare, to find that we lack what we must have to get us through some emergency, let alone rebuild and get back to our normal and comfortable lives. Katrina in New Orleans, 9/11 in New York, massive earthquakes in Los Angeles, Sandy on the East coast. Today, we roll up our own sleeves, and we rebuild ourselves by ourselves. America has never had—indeed, America has never needed—anyone to fall back on. Tomorrow? Who knows? At the moment, we're headed for change, and not for the better. Recall the Soviet Union. Consider Europe today. And did anyone ever think that America's bonds would be downgraded?

We will, however, be spared the humiliation of having to turn to someone else, hat in hand, and ask for help, because there will be no one else. And other countries will know for the first time what it is like to be in a world in which they do not have America to fall back on.

There's a story about Benjamin Franklin that goes like this: In 1787, as the Constitutional Convention was coming to a close, Franklin was asked by a woman what the delegates had accomplished. He said, "We have given you a republic, if you can keep it."

If Franklin were speaking to us today, however, he might say something like this: "In the latter part of the eighteenth century, this country's Founders—and I was honored to be one of them—gave the people of the American colonies a tremendous opportunity to do good, both for themselves and for those who would come after them. Since that time and throughout the intervening years, those who picked up where we left off and carried on our work have built America into something magnificent almost beyond words. I look around this country today, and what I see very nearly takes my breath away. That 'Greatest Generation' that I've heard about comes to mind.

"But now that matters are in your hands, things are looking a bit wobbly. You've let some very important ideas slide away from the national consciousness. This life that you have, this life that you love. You just take it for granted.

"I said to that lady a couple of hundred years ago that we had given her a republic, and thanks to the hard work and heroic sacrifices of the many who came after us and who have gone before you, that republic is still here. But I say to you here at this moment, Can you keep it, can you keep this republic, now that it is in your hands? Frankly, I wonder just a bit."

So might Ben say today.

But is that really where we are? Are we really that close to running out of time? Is it really up to us and us alone? Yes, on all counts, because there really is not a lot of time left, and there is no one else to do what needs to be done. There's just you, as you read these words and think about what they mean, and your fellow Americans.

There also is this to think about: No country other than the United States of America is capable of providing the economic strength and the spiritual and moral leadership to serve as the clear example, the anchor, the rock to cling to that the rest of the world must have, lest it perish.

FOR FURTHER READING

Friedman, Milton, <u>Capitalism & Freedom.</u> Chicago: University of Chicago Press, 1962.

Friedman, Milton & Rose, <u>Free to Choose.</u> New York: Harcourt Brace Jovanovich, 1980.

Friedman, Milton, <u>Money Mischief.</u> New York: Harcourt Brace Jovanovich, 1992.

Gingrich, Newt, <u>A Nation Like No Other.</u> Washington, DC: Regnery Publishing, 2011

Hayek, Friedrich A., <u>The Road to Serfdom.</u> Chicago: University of Chicago Press, 1967.

Simon, William E., <u>A Time for Truth.</u> New York: Berkley Books, 1979.

www.ingramcontent.com/pod-product-compliance
Lightning Source LLC
Chambersburg PA
CBHW070806180526
45168CB00002B/510